Reinhold Niebuhr:

A PROPHETIC VOICE IN OUR TIME

PUBLISHED FOR THE DEAN AND CHAPTER
OF THE CATHEDRAL CHURCH OF ST. JOHN THE DIVINE

Reinhold Niebuhr:
A PROPHETIC VOICE IN OUR TIME

Essays in Tribute by
PAUL TILLICH
JOHN C. BENNETT
HANS J. MORGENTHAU

HAROLD R. LANDON, *Editor*

Wipf and Stock Publishers
150 West Broadway • Eugene OR 97401
2001

Reinhold Niebuhr: A Prophetic Voice in Our Time

By Landon, Harold R.
Copyright©1962 by The Cathedral Church of Saint John the Divine

ISBN: 1-57910-793-1

Reprinted by *Wipf and Stock Publishers*
150 West Broadway • Eugene OR 97401

Previously published by The Seabury Press, 1962.

ACKNOWLEDGMENT

Grateful acknowledgment is made to Charles Scribner's Sons for permission to quote from the published works of Reinhold Niebuhr.

FOREWORD

This book is a compilation of the major papers, with the discussion that followed them, given at the Colloquium in honor of Reinhold Niebuhr on October 20, 1961, at the Cathedral Church of St. John the Divine, New York City. It was my pleasure to open the Colloquium and to welcome the distinguished guests in the remarks that follow.

It is our purpose in this Colloquium to honor one of the great contributors to the thinking of our time. There is not a person in this room who has not been influenced directly or indirectly by Reinhold Niebuhr. Even the man in the street, the ordinary citizen, has been affected by the social and ethical thinking which has grown out of his deep, yet pragmatic piety.

He has been a teacher's teacher in every field of our national life. That he has not always been popular was inevitable. His scorn of secularism is matched by his criticism of the pseudo-liberal sentimentalities of our culture. He has always insisted on the Christian and realistic view which recognizes both the nobility and the misery of man. He made a whole generation of religious, political,

FOREWORD

and economic thinkers relearn the English language. In reminding us that the word *radical* has to do with the fundamental and essential nature of men and things, he has forced us to think clearly about any realistic definition of human dignity. In his thinking neither Marx nor Mrs. Grundy has come out very well.

His profound sense of history led him to see man in his real setting and to know God as one who acts in this history. This has sharpened our whole awareness of what Niebuhr himself describes as the incredibilities of history. We ought also to remember that he himself is one of the splendid incredibilities of our time. It is no small man who could define American conservatism as nothing more than a decadent liberalism, and still end up as the trusted mentor of some of this country's greatest thinkers and leaders in religion, politics, and economics.

But this stimulating, and occasionally irritating mind has a context, and that context is the monumental, gentle, and patient human being which is its visible sacrament. It is as much as because of what he is, as because of what he thinks, that I am privileged to welcome so considerable a number of our country's distinguished leaders to this Colloquium as the guests of our Cathedral Church.

H. W. B. DONEGAN

CONTENTS

Foreword by the Rt. Rev. Horace W. B. Donegan, D.D.,
    Bishop of New York   5
Editor's Introduction   11

Sin and Grace in the Theology of Reinhold Niebuhr
    BY PAUL TILLICH   27
    Discussion   42

Reinhold Niebuhr's Contribution to Christian
Social Ethics
    BY JOHN C. BENNETT   55
    Discussion   80

The Influence of Reinhold Niebuhr in American
Political Life and Thought
    BY HANS J. MORGENTHAU   97
    Discussion   110

The Response of Reinhold Niebuhr   117

Notes   125

Reinhold Niebuhr:

A PROPHETIC VOICE IN OUR TIME

EDITOR'S INTRODUCTION

It is difficult today to convey something of the intellectual ferment and excitement of Union Seminary in the 1930's, when Reinhold Niebuhr was at his prime, and Paul Tillich had just come. It was a moment of fulfilled time, a *kairos*, when suddenly the light of revelation seemed to dawn upon us, and we began to discard the vapid and sentimental illusions that passed for Christianity, and to see something of the depth and profundity of the Christian faith.

It was certainly a time when the winds of doctrine blew hard across Morningside Heights, and Reinhold Niebuhr was at the vortex of that maelstrom of ideas that kept the Seminary in turmoil. The whole spectrum of theological and political opinion was to be seen amongst the faculty and student body. Dr. Tillich has reminded us in this Colloquium that if anyone was *en kairo*, it was Reinhold Niebuhr in the mid-30's.

The inward revolution in thought was matched by the outward pace of events: the anxiety of the Depression was upon us; the Roosevelt administration, in the process of shoring up the shaking foundations of our society, brought a new dimension into American politics; the Nazi tyranny was menacing; the evil of Communism was beginning to show through its utopian mask; and the threat of war became more and more imminent, until finally we were engulfed in it. What a time to live and preach! Reinhold Niebuhr of all men was up to it. By the power of his great mind and out of the depth of his spirit came a vision of the Christian faith that held in its grasp the whole plane of history and saw both the judgment and mercy of God at work in the catastrophic events of our time.

Edinburgh was having its first air raid when Reinhold Niebuhr was concluding the first series of the Gifford Lectures. So absorbed was he in the exposition of *The Nature and Destiny of Man*, that he did not realize till afterwards that his listeners were receiving outward corroboration, in the screaming sirens, of man's tragic destiny. But Reinhold Niebuhr was expounding a faith that is *Beyond Tragedy*, as we see in the remarkable book of sermons by that name, many of which were delivered in Union Seminary Chapel, and which for depth of insight into the social disorder, for keen analysis of the abyss in human nature, for profound apprehension of the greatness of God's mercy which is the only final answer to the human predicament, are unexcelled. He wrote in the Preface:

It is the thesis of these essays that the Christian view of history passes through the sense of the tragic to a hope and an assurance which is 'beyond tragedy'. The cross, which stands at the center of the Christian worldview, reveals both the seriousness of human sin and the purpose and power of God to overcome it. Christianity's view of history is tragic in so far as it recognizes evil as an inevitable concomitant of even the highest spiritual enterprises. It is beyond tragedy in so far as it does not regard evil as inherent in existence itself, but as finally under the dominion of a good God.[1]

Here is the authentic Christian faith in the classic style. These sermons anticipate theological insights which followed much later. For example, the remarkable sermon, "As Deceivers, yet True," is a profound answer to the so-called problem of "demythologization," long before it was called by that name. He says:

For what is true in the Christian religion can be expressed only in symbols which contain a certain degree of provisional and superficial deception. . . .
We are, therefore deceivers, yet true, when we insist that the Christ who died on the cross will come again in power and glory, that he will judge the quick and the dead and will establish his Kingdom. We do not believe that the human enterprise will have a tragic conclusion; but the ground of our hope lies not in human capacity but in divine power and mercy, in the character of the ultimate reality, which carries the human enterprise.[2]

These sermons reveal what is the central intent of Niebuhr's thought and life: he points to the depth of sin in human nature in order that man may be led to the heights of grace. Niebuhr's thought might well be summed up in these words: "Only the infinite pity of God is equal to the infinite pathos of human life." He exposed the universal corruption of sin in human nature, not because he was a pessimist or a cynic, but in order that man's final trust should not be in any human achievement, but only in the greatness and goodness of God.

This is the underlying theme of Niebuhr's teaching and preaching. It is what makes him a prophetic voice in our time. "Yet so great," he has written, "is the power of human pride that again and again, even within terms of the Christian faith, man places his essential trust not in the ultimate character of God but in some achievement of the human spirit."[3]

There are two things that characterize Reinhold Niebuhr above everything else. The one is to be found in the inscription which appeared in one of his early books dedicated to his father who, he said, taught him "that the critical faculty can be united with a reverent spirit." Around these two foci—intelligence and reverence—moves the thought of Reinhold Niebuhr. His mind explored vast reaches of history in search of moral and ethical patterns, and he was able to open up vistas of meaning in wide areas of man's experience hitherto unexplored. "His metier," in the words of his colleague Paul Scherer, "is to work not with miniatures but with murals . . . with the spread of some vast engagements on many fronts, with the impact of worlds, with the panorama of a civilization, with maps of centuries and continents in high relief."[4] To follow the convolutions of his thought through a jungle of ideas without losing the way was often an exhausting exercise. His biographer, June Bingham, in her book *Courage to Change*, says that he is "forever at war with oversimplification." Reinhold Niebuhr's primary vocation, it should never be forgotten, has been to preach the gospel in such a way as to make it credible to modern men. He found meaning and coherence in all that his mind explored. He brought new areas of knowledge in anthropology, psychology, sociology, and history into the context of Christian thought. This is the first basic element in his life and thought.

The second is to be seen in this incident which took

EDITOR'S INTRODUCTION

place at the time of the Gifford Lectures. It may be an apocryphal story, but it is none the less true and illustrates the primary motive of his thought. An elderly devout woman was reported to have said after hearing his lectures on the mysteries of sin and grace, "I dinna ken a word ye say, but I think you make God very great." This is the impression he leaves! His intellectual explorations were always at the service and under the direction of his deep faith.

Reinhold Niebuhr is not only a thinker, but a man of affairs. His advice and counsel has been constantly sought in the highest political circles at home and abroad. In some ways the most remarkable contribution of his life is his last published book, *The Structure of Nations and Empires*. Here he examines the whole sweep of human history to show how the configurations of power in nations and empires seek justice and promote injustice at the same time and make history a continuous battleground in the struggle for power. There are, of course, theological overtones in it. In some ways it simply spells out in terms of the collective life of man what is the basic theme of *The Nature and Destiny of Man*—the universal corruption of human nature which is the taint of sin. The drama of history corroborates the theme clearly stated in one of the Thirty-nine Articles of the Book of Common Prayer: "It is the fault and corruption of the Nature of every man . . . whereby man is very far gone from original righteousness and is of his own nature inclined to evil . . . *and this infection of nature doth remain, yea in them that are regenerated.*"[5] The following passage from *The Structure of Nations and Empires* illustrates this:

15

HAROLD R. LANDON

History is a realm in which human freedom and natural necessity are curiously intermingled. Man's freedom constantly creates the most curious and unexpected and unpredictable emergences and emergencies in history. . . . But without an empirical inquiry into the relation between the contingent and the permanent forces of community, each generation is tempted to exalt some particular instrument of justice, which has succeeded in a given instance, as the absolutely essential instrument of justice; or to attribute injustice to some particular institution or policy which has been the particular cause of particular evils, but is falsely understood if interpreted as the final cause of all social evil.

Our best hope of a tolerable political harmony and of an inner peace rests upon our ability to observe the limits of human freedom, even while we responsibly exploit its creative possibilities.[6]

For breadth of mind and grasp of history, this book is comparable to Toynbee's *Study of History*. It is an attempt at a philosophy of history from a Christian point of view.

This brings us to the "continuing dialogue" with his great friend and colleague, Paul Tillich. When Hitler removed Paul Tillich from his professorship (Tillich says he had the honor to be the first Christian professor so to be removed), he did American theology an incalculable service, for thus began one of the most interesting collaborations in the history of Christian thought. We felt at that time that these men both spoke the same theological language (even when they did not use the same terms) and moreover had a deep kinship in the hidden recesses of the spirit, which it has taken these three decades fully to spell out.

The impact of these two men in American theology has been so great that the focus of attention in theology

EDITOR'S INTRODUCTION

is now divided between Europe and America. Seldom have two men who are so creative in thought had the opportunity for such an intimate dialectic over the course of so many years. It has been an intensely fruitful exchange, and we are fortunate that so much of it has been made public.

One of the interesting things which this Colloquium reveals is that Paul Tillich and Reinhold Niebuhr are closer to each other than to their critics, and what is surprising is not so much their differences as their similarities. In Dr. Tillich's remarkable reply to Dr. John MacKay (which is the last question and answer in the discussion following Dr. Tillich's lecture) we see the essential agreement at the very heart of their theology. Reinhold Niebuhr's section in *The Nature and Destiny of Man* entitled "Grace as Power in, and Mercy Towards, Man" is a permanent contribution to theological writing. Nowhere is more clearly set forth the ambiguity of sin and grace in the human personality. It is Reinhold Niebuhr's central concern to show the universality of sin in human nature which corrupts man's highest achievements, even at the pinnacle of grace. Dr. Tillich's answer to Dr. MacKay shows how completely they are in agreement on this point.

Indeed, one could say that no concern has been more in evidence in Reinhold Niebuhr than to point again and again in all his profound analyses of the human situation to the Protestant Principle which Paul Tillich has formulated thus:

The central principle of Protestantism is the doctrine of justification by grace alone, which means that no individual and no human group can claim a divine dignity for its moral achievements, for its sacramental power, for its sanctity, for its doctrine. Protestantism requires that they be challenged by the prophetic protest, which gives God alone sanctity and denies every claim of human pride. This protest against itself on the experience of God's majesty, constitutes the Protestant Principle.[7]

When Paul Tillich says in the course of his answer to Dr. MacKay: "I don't know how far Niebuhr was also influenced on this point by the Barthian school; even the Divine Spirit, who in Christian tradition is that which is working in us, cannot be experienced so that we can say 'I have it.' We can only say 'I believe that I believe,' 'I have faith that I have faith,' as you can never say directly, 'I have faith,' or 'I have the Spirit.' Now here we are at a point where the dialectics almost never come down to earth, and if I understand you rightly, then you have expressed at this moment a criticism which is against my own theological structure, but from which I don't know the way out, in view of the realism about the human predicament which I share with Niebuhr." This is so like Reinhold Niebuhr!

On this point Reinhold Niebuhr quotes Paul Tillich in *The Nature and Destiny of Man* in that chapter which deals with the paradox of "Having and Not Having the Truth." The quotation is to the effect that we must submit the idea of justification by faith to the experience of justification by faith. When a man does this he discovers in all humility that the truth is that we do not possess the truth. Here Niebuhr and Tillich are so close in their thinking that they can both quote from each other.

In one of his sermons, Tillich speaks of that matchless painting of John the Baptist by Matthias Grünewald in which the painter shows John pointing with his finger to Jesus Christ. "There his whole being is in the finger with which he points to the cross. This is the greatest symbol of which I know for the true authority of the Church and the Bible. They should not point to themselves but to the reality which breaks again and again through the established forms of their authority and through the heart and form of our personal experience."[8]

This is exactly what Reinhold Niebuhr always attempted to do: his seeming preoccupation with the universal taint of sin in all man's achievements was but the other side of his pointing to him in whom there was no sin. This is the central motive of his life and his thought; to point to the sinfulness of man only that thus man may be ready to receive the Divine Redeemer. Here is a characteristic passage in which this is revealed:

There is no conceivable society in which the pride of the community and the arrogance of its oligarchs must not be resisted. It is possible to offer this resistance at times in the name of some minority interest. But the final resistance must come from the community which knows and worships a God to whom all nations are subject. Sometimes the testimony of the prophet of this God speaks in a common voice with the criticism of political minorities; it may on occasion be very necessary that the two types of defiance be joined. Yet they are never one and the same thing. The Christian Church must be and remain a fellowship of Christians, and *Christ is the judge of the self-will and self-righteousness of every social group.*

Reinhold Niebuhr is criticised for not having a more explicit ecclesiology. The reason for this is clear: it was not his vocation as a prophet who spoke both for and against the Church. Reinhold Niebuhr saw so clearly the sinfulness of the redeemed man, that he was wary of any theological formulation which allowed room for human pride to creep in the back door, even if that back door be the Church. "Moral contrition is the human foundation of the Church, but God's grace is its completion."[9] Few men have written more incisively about the Church than does Niebuhr in this passage:

> The Church is that place in human society where men are disturbed by the word of the eternal God which stands as a judgment upon human aspirations. But it is also the place where the word of mercy, reconciliation and consolation is heard . . . Here human incompleteness is transcended though not abolished. Here human sin is overcome by the divine mercy, though man remains a sinner. No church can lift man out of the partial and finite history in which all human life stands. Every interpretation of the church which promises an 'efficient grace' by which man ceases to be man and enters prematurely into the kingdom of God is a snare and a delusion. The Church is not the kingdom of God. The Church is the place in human society where the kingdom of God impinges upon all human enterprises through the divine word, and where the grace of God is made available to those who have accepted his judgment.[10]

It is true of both Reinhold Niebuhr and Paul Tillich that they have often spoken to those groups in our society and culture which Paul Tillich calls the *latent church*. For Paul Tillich writes, "There is a church latent in all history and culture. This insight is deadly for all ecclesiastical and theological arrogance."[11] It may be true that there is a certain lack in Reinhold Niebuhr in his doctrine of the Church, and yet no one in our generation has served the Church more faithfully, made its doctrine more relevant, its theology more understandable, its message more available, its ethic more challenging, its life more authentic and real, and recalled the Church more nearly to herself than Reinhold Niebuhr.

While no one insists more strongly on the pervasiveness of sin and its universal manifestation in the whole of man's history, culture, and personality than Reinhold Niebuhr, he remains unwilling to accept the ontological terms of Paul Tillich to describe sin. This is perhaps a logical inconsistency in his thought, for if sin is a universal fact, it is natural that man should seek some explanation of what Paul Tillich calls "the transition from essence to existence universally." And if Reinhold Niebuhr is willing to say (as Paul Tillich quotes him in this Colloquium) that we should no longer use such words as *original sin* but should replace them by terms something like *universal estrangement* then a movement of thought in the direction of ontology would seem to be inevitable. When Tillich uses such a phrase as "sin is a fact before it is an act," Reinhold Niebuhr is afraid that man's sense of responsibility for this act may be lost in his acceptance of it as a fact. Yet there is healing in the mere recognition of the fact that sin is man's universal destiny, and when Paul Tillich writes, "Salvation is healing from the cosmic disease that prevents love," there is somehow the beginning of grace in the mere acceptance of this as a fact.

Perhaps it should be recognized that both Reinhold Niebuhr and Paul Tillich are right at this point, and that the witness of both is needed as the necessary corrective of the one to the other. For if one accepts the analysis of the existential situation as seen by Niebuhr and Tillich, it is inevitable to try and relate this to the nature of ultimate reality as Tillich does in his ontological descriptions;

but having done so, the danger which Reinhold Niebuhr sees of depersonalizing the Christian message and robbing man of his sense of personal responsibility for sin becomes real, and his warning relevant. At this point they are both in agreement and disagreement; and the mixture of agreement and disagreement is important and should be maintained.

Reinhold Niebuhr is criticized in this Colloquium for "lack of vision." This criticism, however, is based on a misunderstanding of the vocation of Reinhold Niebuhr. He never felt it was his responsibility as a teacher of Christian Ethics and as a prophetic voice to give any kind of blueprint for society. He preferred to maintain the tension of what he called the "impossible possibility" of the absolute love command of the Gospel, even though man's social life or group behavior demands some more practicable guides. His real vision, strangely enough, is that of the community of grace, the Church, where man receives the word that both judges and redeems, the place, to use Dr. Tillich's language, where man "accepts that he is accepted though unacceptable." It is fascinating that Niebuhr should say of the contemporary existentialists, as quoted by Dr. Tillich, "What they cannot accept is that they are accepted, namely, forgiveness and grace." His vision of the community of grace which is the Church is not fully spelled out in a doctrine of the Church. For Reinhold Niebuhr the Church is not the kingdom of God, even though he might perhaps be willing to say that the Church is a sacrament of the kingdom.

On the basis of three years experience of teaching at a theological school in East Africa, I can say that nothing is more needed in the Church in Africa, and I believe in the so called uncommitted nations of the world, as the prophetic vision and understanding of Reinhold Niebuhr. The explosions which are blowing the white man out of so much of Africa and Asia are nothing but the reaction of the so called primitive people to the arrogance and will-to-power of the representatives of Western culture, an arrogance which is compounded of the pride not only of the white man but also of the Christian man. Here we see the profound truth of a characteristic statement by Reinhold Niebuhr: "There is an element of positive evil in the most virtuous life." We have to remember that some of the worst racist policies and practices are the product of those who are avowedly Christian. It is this message of the profound truth of Christian faith which will enable Reinhold Niebuhr to be heard on this and the other side of not only the Iron Curtain, but the Color Curtain, or whatever separates man from his true humanity. He has established the relevance of the Christian message for the problems of our age and of every age.

In the closing chapters of *Moral Man and Immoral Society* Niebuhr has a vision and writes thus:

Yet there is beauty in our tragedy. We are, at least, rid of some of our illusions. We can no longer buy the highest satisfaction of the individual life at the expense of social injustice. We cannot build our individual ladders to heaven and leave the total human enterprise unredeemed of its successes and corruptions. In the task of that redemption, the most effective agents will be men who have substituted some new illusions for the abandoned ones. The most important of these illusions is that the collective life of mankind can achieve perfect justice. It is a very valuable illusion for the moment, for justice cannot be approximated if the hope of its perfect realization does not generate a sublime madness in the soul. Nothing but such madness will do battle with malignant powers and spiritual wickedness in high places. The illusion is dangerous because it encourages terrible fanaticism. It must, therefore, be brought under the control of reason. One can only hope that reason will not destroy it before its work is done.[12]

Here surely is sublime vision in which again we see the highest critical faculty under the control of a deeply reverent spirit.

Reinhold Niebuhr was for more than thirty years a teacher, and part of the rich legacy he left behind is a whole generation of students who remember him above all as a human being so free of pretence, so honest in soul, so humble in mind, so reverent in spirit. His sister, Hulda Niebuhr, has a book of stories for children with the title, *Greatness Passing By*. The participants in the Reinhold Niebuhr Colloquium, as well as countless men and women who knew Reinhold Niebuhr, apply to him the words of John Drinkwater's poem, "Those who worship greatness passing by, themselves are great." Those of us who knew and loved Reinhold Niebuhr knew a great human being who changed the climate of theology and who spoke with the power of a prophet in our time. He has given us his own fine statement of the test of true prophecy:

All of us will always have something of the false prophet in us, wherefore we ought to speak humbly. We will mistake our own dreams for the word of God. Sometimes sloth will tempt us to make a superficial analysis of the moral and social facts with which we are dealing; sometimes pride will tempt us to speak as if we had already attained or were already made perfect;

sometimes cowardice will tempt us to make concessions to the immense, blind and stubborn self-righteousness with which every culture, every nation and every individual wards off the word of God.

Thus the Church can disturb the security of sinners, only if it is not itself too secure in its belief that it has the word of God. The prophet himself stands under the judgment which he preaches. If he does not know that, he is a false prophet.[13]

HAROLD R. LANDON

PAUL TILLICH:

*Sin and Grace in the Theology
of Reinhold Niebuhr*

PAUL TILLICH:

Mr. Chairman and Friends: I must really say "Friends." I rarely have had such an assembly of friends which I found in the first (and now almost 30) years that I am in this country. And now all of them are here.

I consider it a great honor and at the same time a great joy to participate in this meeting. When I thought about the possibilities for such a speech, it proved to be an impossible task if it had to be done in the way of an ordinary speech. So I decided not to give an ordinary speech, and not to tell you what you all know much better: namely, Reinhold Niebuhr's theology, and especially his doctrine of sin, guilt, and grace. But I decided to ask you to participate with me in our personal encounter—personal in the sense of an exchange of thoughts about these and related subjects which is now, indeed, going on for almost 30 years.

I look back in this moment to a telephone call which came to me in my preliminary place of exile in July, 1933, at the Baltic Sea, and on the other side of the telephone was Reinhold Niebuhr, of whom I only knew the name because his brother had just translated my book *The Re-*

ligious Situation. And he asked me to come to America, because he had read in the newspapers that I was deprived of my position. And then, after much hesitation, I came in November of the same year.

I was received in Union. All of the Union professors had given a little of their old furniture in the apartment which now the doctor has—by far the largest—I always had the feeling that I was in the apartment of the Bishop of New York and not of a little professor. In any case, I do not forget this. I want to mention that the first human being who greeted us in Union Seminary was Mrs. Niebuhr.

Then I remember our walks along Riverside Drive in the two years in which Reinie worked on his *magnum opus, The Nature and Destiny of Man,* and we talked about many of the problems which then came in such a wonderful way into this great book. We two at that time were characterized as the intruders of neo-orthodoxy into the beautiful life of American liberal theology, and I still find in some provincial little magazines that I am characterized in memory of these years as neo-orthodox.

In any case, we worked together, we talked together, we lived nearly together. But we also developed independently of each other, and slowly the different characteristics became clearer and sharper. His background was a social-ethical passion from the very beginning of his ministerial work in a parish. My development, on the basis of the German background and German classical philosophy, went in another direction, more in the individual, psychological, and metaphysical, or ontological direction. This different basic interest, this fundamental difference in the structure of our being, came out also in those controversies which we had in public: my criticism of his book and his criticism of my book *Systematic Theology*. Our conversation developed, as a good conversation should, in a mixture of agreement and disagreement. Since the subject I am to speak about is that point in which there is the most agreement and disagreement, the concept of sin, I want to concentrate mostly on this. Grace is a concept in which I do not see much to discuss between him and me; but about sin and guilt we had conversations which have lasted now many years.

And now back to our common start in and after the First World War. What had grasped both of us was the human situation seen in the light of the political and social catastrophes which we in central Europe experienced directly, and certainly existentially, as one says today. But he, with his ability of empathetic participation in far removed historical events, was with us at that time, although we did not know him and we did not know that he was with us. Our problem at that time was to find the way between the Social Democratic utopianism on the one hand, which was unaware of the human situation of man's existential estrangement and the ecclesiastical, the Lutheran transcendentalism, on the other hand, which was aware, certainly, of the human situation, but did not believe that this situation allows any transformation. And between these two poles we stood when we came out of the First World War: between the movement for social justice represented by the Social Democratic Party and the movement in the merely vertical direction represented by the Lutheran churches.

In this country the situation was different. There was the social gospel theology. There was the effect the 18th century still had on this country in the beginning of the 20th century (much more than it did in Germany). There was the problem of liberal thinking with respect to the human predicament. Both problems were very near to each other; and so it was possible that Richard Niebuhr, when he read my book *The Religious Situation,* which appeared about 1926, translated it, and this was the forerunner of my friendship also with Reinhold Niebuhr. Our work in Germany, our Religious Socialist movement, was at that time a limited success. Later on it became, especially in present-day Germany, and also in other countries, indirectly a success. But at that time it was very much hidden, very small, and then removed by Hitler immediately. But what happened here is in some way a real success story (if you want to use this disagreeable word) namely, the way in which this one man, Reinhold Niebuhr, was able to change the pacifist mood, the liberal theological attitude, the so-called scientific theology, and introduce something entirely new for the situation as he found it. This occurred almost suddenly. It was about ten years after the same thing had happened in Germany. With the death of Harnack and Troeltsch, suddenly the theology which up to this time had ruled many German faculties lost any actual influence. It simply disappeared under the tremendous impact of the Barthian theology, or it went into the underground. When I remember what happened here, it was similarly astonishing. When I came, everybody asked only one question—whatever was discussed theologically—namely the question, "What do you think about pacifism?" When I gave a lecture on the Trinity, or on the Biblical studies in the Fourth Gospel, immediately when the discussion started a student got up and asked, "What do you think about pacifism?" Of course I was hesitating on this point, because I never was and even now am not a pacifist. This disappeared after Reinie had made his tremendous attack. This question went into the background and it was replaced by the problem of the human predicament. Now I cannot evaluate this. I believe it was absolutely necessary, and I tried to support him as much as I could in my lectures and early writings; but he was the man who changed the climate in an almost sudden way.

Then we both tried to systematize our thought, to organize it, and the difference of methods came out. He is basically a Biblicist, not in the bad sense, but in the sense that all his writings continuously refer to the Biblical foundations of the Christian faith, and especially of the doctrine of man. He has a rather low evaluation of the non-Biblical literature, especially if this literature has the bad luck to have been written by a philosopher from Plato on. He has a special method of dealing with representatives of Western philosophy, a method which one perhaps could call the critical-comparing method. He quotes a passage of Paul, and then in opposition to it a passage of Plato, or of Spinoza, or even worse, of Hegel; and then he says: "Now here you have the Biblical truth and there you have the philosophical error." When I read the first volume, *The Nature and Destiny of Man,* in which the problem of sin is mostly discussed, I was surprised to find so often this word *error;* and I think if Niebuhr would ask himself now whether it is justified in the light of his evaluation of the human predicament, in which the Biblical theologian also happens to be, to call philosophical opinions simply and directly and unambiguously error. I believe he would say, "Yes, this was an error!" Now (since I compare myself) let me say what I think we should do with the writings of philosophers and other men of the past. I would here reintroduce the concept *Kairos*, the right time, which is a very difficult one and has been criticized, especially in view of the historical events after the early 20's of this century. If we deal with sayings of the classical philosophers from Socrates till the present— I would go a little bit farther back to my beloved Parmenides—we should first of all show that they have written *en kairo*, that their writings cannot simply be taken out of the total historical situation in which they were created. The dialectics of history itself partly refuted them, partly preserved them. This is dialectical thinking; this is not thinking in the method of critical-comparison between what is true and what is error.

Here you see one very interesting point in which I understood why I never was satisfied with Niebuhr's treatment of philosophers. They were not seen *en kairo;* they were seen only *ex contrario,* i.e., out of the opposite. Now, of course, this has consequences. A week ago we had a wonderful talk in Cambridge for one to two hours, and he said to me quite spontaneously, "I have accepted your point of view in this respect. We cannot use any longer the language of the tradition if we want to communicate anything to the people of our time." As an example, he gave me his use of the words *sin,* and especially *original sin,* in his book. For me this was a confirmation of my very desperate, difficult, and often failing attempt to use another language than the traditional, especially (and here I agree fully with him) with respect to these words. The words *original sin* shouldn't be used at all. He accepted—if I understood him rightly—something like *universal estrangement* instead of the term *original* or *hereditary sin.* But this is an expression of something in him about which I will speak later on. In his age and bodily weakness, he is still able to translate his own earlier language, or at least, is trying to do it. This is one point.

A second point was his attitude toward Existentialism. You know that his books start with a description of the easy conscience of modern man. He described this in all the different ways; and now he has seen that the underground of this seemingly easy conscience—which for a long time and always in some places was a very uneasy conscience—has come into the foreground and become visible in the whole Existentialist literature. He says: "I know this now; we cannot speak so easily any longer of an easy conscience. One thing is lacking in all this literature. They are unwilling to accept—not so much my descriptions of the human predicament if only these terrible words are removed—that they are accepted, to accept forgiveness and grace, and the possibility of transformation." This I heard from him for the first time last week when he said: "The difficulty at present is not so much to bring modern man to the acknowledgment of his estrangement and predicament, but it is much more to bring him to the *in-spite-of* in the message of Justification." I can only say that I believe that this is a very profound and true affirmation.

The only question I would have here is: Isn't there also in these men—let us think not of a bad philosopher, but of a good novelist on the human predicament, namely, Kafka—isn't there also in his description of man's predicament common grace, a hidden grace, effective? Why is it possible that in the last ten years Kafka has become the saint of all the colleges and universities where I had the privilege to speak? Because he has the grace to show these students, who perhaps had that easy conscience of which Niebuhr speaks so often, that they have no justification for such an easy conscience. As Luther always said, the beginning of grace is the hell of repentance, of awareness of what one is. So I would say in these men there is the beginning of grace. But I don't know whether Niebuhr would go as far as that.

Then I come to the most controversial point between us: namely, his rejection of all kinds of ontology (if applied to Christianity of course). I don't want to speak about this in general terms, but in terms of his doctrine of sin. What is so interesting is that which I find so often in all anti-philosophical theologians: in the moment in which they start speaking and using abstract terms, they immediately become ontologists against their own will. I prefer to be an ontologist with my will, because then you can avoid things.

Even here something happened in our talk which was very interesting. Often I have bothered him with his word, "Sin is not necessary but inevitable." Now this is

SIN AND GRACE

logical nonsense, and that is just what he told me! "But," he said, "this logical nonsense we have to take." Here I agree with him, only I wouldn't call it logical nonsense. I would say that it is the right description of the polarity of freedom and destiny in which we all find ourselves, and which even support each other as polarities always do. We cannot be free without destiny; we cannot have destiny without freedom. If you bring this conflict down to necessity and contingency, then, of course, it is logical nonsense. *Necessity* and *contingency* are terms which belong to natural science. If we come to a description of the human situation, as we are aware of it in ourselves, then we must describe it in this double way. So I would, and did very often, accept his term *inevitable*. Then it is necessary to say, "This is not an escape from ontology, but what is behind it is good ontology: namely, the unity of universal destiny combined with personal freedom and responsibility." And that is what he really wants, to avoid implying that sin is something essential. And here again I was astonished. How often he uses this word *essential* which I remember from my school education is a very old classical word of ontology, or as it was formerly called, metaphysics. How impossible it is to escape ontology if you try to make any Christian doctrine understandable at all! Here is his realism, which gives him the Augustinian and Protestant position of inevitability, and his moral seriousness which makes him emphasize responsibility. But he still did not like my phrase, *transition from essence to existence universally*. I do not like it either, and forbid my students all the time to use it in their sermons. But nevertheless, I think as an analytic term, it is quite adequate to the situation and not different from what Niebuhr means.

There are other particular problems in which ontology breaks through in him. Here again something came out in our speech a week ago. He derives sin basically from pride. There is no word in all his writings and preaching which is more often used than the word *pride*. Since the appearance of his book I have always said: the word *pride* is a particular moral category, while *hubris,* the Greek for self-elevation, what he really wants to say, is an ontological category and refers to the whole of man. To my surprise, even without talking about this problem, he spontaneously told me, "This is the other point in which you were right. I should not have called it pride, because this is a particular moral category, and we have to understand it in a much more universal way." But this means that the moment he uses a term like *self-elevation,* or the Greek word *hubris* in its original meaning, we are in the midst of ontology; and it is really great to realize how open he is in this respect.

Another point: in his book *The Self and the Dramas of History,* he says: "Here is something which is beyond any ontology, namely the self." But to define ontology in this connection he uses Aristotle's definition of man as rational structure. But he defines reason in a much narrower way than Aristotle or classical theology. It is what I call the "calculating" reason, or the "technical" reason. It is not the *logos* type of reason. And, of course, if you do this, then this is much too little. But when we use the word *self,* we use an ontological category, and a very fundamental ontological category of highest importance:

namely, the ontological fact that man is the only completely centered being, and alone has a completely centered self. So here again, in order to say something with which we can for the most part perhaps agree, he uses ontology and cannot escape it.

Then I come to the problem of the relation of sin to nature. Now you know, perhaps, that Niebuhr and I often walked through nature. It was mostly Riverside Park, but anyhow there are some very beautiful trees; and while he developed his future big book, I sometimes was deviated by a tree, or the river, or clouds behind it, and suddenly I noticed he didn't care for this at all. When I told him that I cared for this, he called me a German Romanticist. Now this very nice controversy has much deeper philosophical implications. It has the implication that the relationship of nature and sin is seen by him in a way which makes nature simply innocent. This makes it impossible to understand why nature in man is certainly not innocent, and how nature in man can be saved, if nature universally cannot be saved. This whole vision, which we have in many of the specially Deutero-Paulinian writings but also in his genuine writings, this vision of the belongingness of nature and man, is something which I missed in our discussions. So he said, against all mythology, that one should not use animal symbols, like wolf or others, for aggressive human instincts. But I think the myth is right in doing it, because we are all this also; all levels of reality are in us, and if the whole of these levels does not stand under the problem of grace, I do not see how you can isolate man. In the social respect, he never does it. There he sees what the power structure is, and he never makes this distinction. In individual life he has still—I have the feeling—a remnant of liberal Pelagianism in that he separates man so strongly from nature.

Very interesting are his statements about man and the natural necessity of death. Here he is a better ontologist than Paul, and he knows this and turns against Paul with respect to the relationship of sin and death. Paul is ambiguous at this point, but in any case there are words in which it seems as if Paul derives death from sin; and Niebuhr—again in a deep ontological insight—knows that death belongs to finitude, and that the conquest of death is given to man only as a particular gift on the basis of his relationship to God. Therefore I am very glad that at this point he denies the superstitious idea that man's spirituality changes the ontological structure of nature.

But there are other elements: for instance, the unity of body and soul, which as a good Old Testament scholar he always emphasizes, rejecting the pseudo-Platonic (Plato was much better than this) idea of the immortality of the soul. But in any case, here again we must ask the question, What does this mean if you don't speak of the immortality of the soul? What does eternal life then mean? And this is not so easy in view of the fact that we are dying.

Then something which surprised me: the doctrine of the Fall with the transhuman elements in it. Here he becomes completely cosmological—that means also a special form of ontology.

Here he goes into angelology. (That's too difficult for me, not only the idea but also the word. Much easier for me is the idea and the word *satanology*.) And it's very interesting that he also says that man is not the cause of sin. Here other more embracing structures are effective, but not in such a way that they force man. Niebuhr always keeps responsibility, but he has this vision; and, therefore I don't understand rightly why he criticizes Kant's doctrine of the perversion of the will in the transcendence. This is what Kant really wanted to say: the transcendent fall. It is not a literalistic myth, but something which shows the universality in which all beings are.

Now this is enough; I was only asked to give a few ideas about the basic attitude of Reinie. I basically agree with his description of human predicament. I do not agree with special points of theological formulations with respect to the doctrine of man. But it was a great experience, and decisive for my own development, to have this ever on-going talk with him as a friend.

Here I admire something, and want to close with this: the mixture of a definite structure with admirable flexibility in a man of his age, his character, and his creativity. He has at the same time a clear profile and a remaining openness. Few better things can be said of a man of his achievement, his work, and his age. My only hope is that these living dialectics will go on for a long time.

DISCUSSION:

Question (Dr. John Hutchison): Professor Tillich, to press you a little further on your own use of the word *ontological,* particularly in relation to Niebuhr's argument on that point, I have a feeling that he has rejected the word as you have used it sometimes, when he has felt that it has been a particular kind of ontology—namely, Neo-Platonic. The word *ontology* covers a lot of different kinds of metaphysics and ontologies, and perhaps in his attacks upon you he has been concentrating on what he has thought to be your preoccupation with a particular ontology.

Professor Tillich: I am not so sure about that. We have discussed that point, for instance, in the transition from essence to existence, where he uses the word *essence* and in other places *existence* and *predicament.* I don't see that he criticizes me here (Charles Hartshorne[1] always does) from the point of view that I am too static, as against his philosophy of becoming which he has from Whitehead. It's not this kind of difference. I haven't found in his writing any philosopher who does not fall into the errors which he refutes. That seems to me to speak more for the general rejection of this kind of language. Of course, if it were simply Parmenidean against Heraclitean, then we could easily come to terms, because he wouldn't go as far as Whitehead and Hartshorne to speak of the developing God. But the difference is more than this. He has the feeling and, I think, believes that ontology depersonalizes the whole Christian message. Of course, it would do so if the living symbols were abolished by abstract terminology. But what theologians have done, if they used philosophical concepts, was not to replace the symbols but to interpret them, to make the symbols clear to those categories of our understanding with which we are able to grasp the meaning of symbols, and of this he is afraid, of course.

Question (Professor Wilhelm Pauck): Isn't the opposition to ontology, on the part of a man like Niebuhr, more an opposition to the system, to the tendency on the part of the metaphysician to want to say something about everything, so that the whole universe, the whole cosmos is somehow penetrated by this reason, or whatever it is that the ontologist or the metaphysician uses to explain the mysteries of life? And the opposition of Niebuhr is against the pretension, the presumptuousness, the *hubris*, the pride of the system in the ontologist and the metaphysician, and not so much to their language. Therefore, Niebuhr can use metaphysical, ontological terms even from different kinds of philosophical and metaphysical systems. But that he does use this language and these terms does not imply that he is an ontologist, therefore, or must become an ontologist under the compulsion to develop a system, i.e., to say something coherent about everything, from God who is all in all to himself.

Professor Tillich: Now I have the feeling that Niebuhr has not one tenth of the passion against the system which you revealed in the way in which you spoke of it. In his *magnum opus* (*The Nature and Destiny of Man*) he speaks about many things. Although he has not three volumes of systematic theology as I hope to have, he has two volumes as I also have at present.

Question (Professor Richard Kroner): I am also a little bewildered when you always talk about ontology. You know when you came, you told me that I should never forget the Bible and the Biblical God. Then I was the philosopher and you were the theologian. [*Professor Tillich:* We turned around.] I am a little bewildered that the word *ontology* was not used by philosophers after Kant. Kant was supposed to have killed forever the very possibility of ontology. Kant was using epistemology, ethics, and philosophy of religion and philosophy of history in place of ontology. In any case, philosophy was concerned with subject and not with being as such. Why do you now use the word *ontology* so much? Are you influenced by Heidegger perhaps? Heidegger had a special reason for reintroducing being into philosophy. I have the feeling that you use the word *ontology* as almost equivalent to the word *philosophy,* or the word *metaphysics,* or to any branch of philosophy in contrast with theology. Niebuhr is right when he defends the ethical or moral meaning of sin against you. You make it too much cosmologic, but I wouldn't enter into this.

Professor Tillich: First of all, your suspicion is justified. I think Heidegger has indeed reintroduced the term *ontology* as a fundamental part of philosophy, not identical with all philosophy but only with the fundamental part; and I was very glad for this, because the word *metaphysics* cannot be used in this country. Metaphysics means looking at the clouds: *meta—above* the physical world. This has nothing to do with the real meaning of the word *metaphysics,* but this is the popular understanding or misunderstanding of the word *metaphysics,* even in high academic circles. For this reason of communication I avoid the word *metaphysics.* Perhaps one day this is no longer necessary; but for the time being I am very glad that many people who wouldn't dare to use the word *metaphysics* any more, because that would bring them into this trans-nebular realm, use the word *ontology.* They know that simply means an analysis of the structure and character of being—being-as-such, and not special realms of being. That is indeed what I mean, and in this I confess I am much nearer to my Catholic friends and critics of my theology (like Father Weigel and others) than to those Protestants who come out of the Ritschlian school.

Question (Professor Jacob Taubes): The remarks of Professor Pauck and Professor Kroner remind me of George Bernard Shaw's saying: the news about the death of ontology is greatly exaggerated. You know that that was once the case when the news passed around that he died. He wrote a letter to *The Times* saying "It's greatly exaggerated." And I think I am forced to take sides here with Professor Tillich. Obviously, if we say anything, for example, that the self is X or Y, we are making a statement about the self as a being and, therefore, you have the ontological question. Surely—and that's the point at which I would like to ask for clarification—I think that Professor Tillich and Heidegger would be the first ones to acknowledge it—to speak about being in relation to the self demands different categories than in speaking about nature. The ancient ontology, the ontology of the classics, is metaphysics. I would like to ask, and this is a question to you, Professor Tillich, whether modern ontology, starting already from Kant on is not in a sense meta-historical—if we may use the word *meta-history* in the same way as the ancients used the term *metaphysics* after Aristotle.

Professor Tillich: Yes, I would accept this suggestion very gladly. But I would say that as the Greeks had their pre-Augustinian interpretation of history in spite of their metaphysics, so we cannot have meta-history without also having metaphysics.

Question (Professor Henry Nelson Wieman): I may not understand you, Professor Tillich, but in the way that I do understand you, you identify God with being. Being cannot be characterized; to characterize it in any way it becomes a kind of being. Therefore, when God is characterized in any way, he becomes a symbol of being-itself; being-itself is unknowable because it can have no character whatsoever and, therefore, God is not knowable except in the form of a symbol which represents the unknowable. Am I right?

Professor Tillich: Yes, but you are not right when you say, as so many people said in criticism, that I identify God with being. I say that the first question of every child, and of every undistorted philosopher who still has the metaphysical quality of the naive child, every such human being asks when he hears about God and starts to think, "Is God?" What does it mean when we say that God is? To this question I answer: You can never say that he is *a* being. If you ask this question you must say with respect to the problem of being, he is being-itself. He is *esse qua esse*. Here I am in the scholastic tradition. That is the first thing. But this is not the whole thing and, therefore, the word *identification* is a word invented not by you but by others for polemical reasons. What I really say about God, first, is that he is life; and the word *life* has much more weight in the description than the word *being*. And then I say he is spirit. And then I say he is related, and so on. This traditional classical statement that the question of the being of God must be answered by the formula that he is not a being but being-itself, the power of being in all being—this simple thing was a shock for the nominalistic tradition in which most universities and theological schools find themselves. For this reason this question played such a role. But we shouldn't go to my thinking, but to Niebuhr's.

Question (Dr. John Hutchison): What happened to sin? Is that an ontological category in the terms with which you have now characterized ontology? Can you handle sin as an ontological category?

Professor Tillich: Yes, now I will tell you what my teacher Martin Kähler said. He defines sin as *wiesen wiedernichtkeit* which means "contradiction to essence." And I am convinced that this went deep into my unconscious, and that out of this much of this idea came. In this sense I would say, "Yes." But when we come to the question, What is the essence which we contradict? then this essence is amongst others the polarity of freedom and destiny, including therefore responsibility and tragedy, and so on.

Question (Professor Daniel Williams): Is there not, Dr. Tillich, another facet of the difference between your method and Niebuhr's? It seems to me it is not the question of system, not even the question about reason, but a strong tendency on his part to rely on a kind of intuition, or insight, or immediate appropriation of revelation as something given, which breaks through all ordinary categories; whereas in your view revelation is something more general, more open to rational reflection in ontological terms. I'm thinking about the influence on Dr. Niebuhr of Unamuno, which he records in those early dialogues, and the paradoxical, the super-rational character of revelation. What I should like to ask you is: How far do you agree with this? Is ontology possible without revelation? Does ontological reflection itself depend upon a kind of revelation? It seems to me that one kind of answer puts you much farther from Niebuhr, and another kind of answer would put you much closer—if you both depend on something transrational, something given, in order to arrive at ontological truth at all.

Professor Tillich: If I understood you rightly, then I believe that I could say with Niebuhr that revelatory experiences underlie all cultures and religions. I would probably say this. But after having said this, I would say, Let's try to describe phenomenologically such revelatory experiences. How do they look? Here I would go much farther than he does, and than Barth does. I think I told you about a talk I had last July with Karl Barth in Basle. After his daughter-in-law heard my lectures in Chicago she said: "Now I understand what the difference is between Barth and you. You start from below, namely, from the human situation and go up; and he starts from above, he starts with the Trinity immediately in the first volume, and then goes down as much as possible." I was very much impressed by this description because I felt there was a basic truth in it. When I told this to Karl Barth, he was equally struck. He was absolutely excited about it and said, "Yes, I start from above, I have a vision as if a light came from above, and there I start." This is probably the meaning of your question, or at least part of it. Now I don't deny Barth's way of beginning as a possibility. I think it's unsound theology, but certainly its religiously possible. When we start from the human situation and first ask the question, then I have always said, "The answer can never be derived from the question just because of man's existential situation." We must also have the experience which I call revelatory in a universal sense. I believe that all culture and religion is based on such revelatory experiences. And if you ask about ontology, then I believe it was the revelatory experiences, which are beautifully described, for instance, in Walter Otto's (not Rudolph Otto's) description of the gods of Greece and the coming of Dionysius, out of which Greek culture came. Here you see how revelatory experience grasped in an ecstatic way a nation, and out of this, the great Greek philosophy could develop. In this sense I would say there is first a revelatory experience. The ontological analysis and description of it is something which is based on revelatory experience. Such categories as being and becoming, as in Parmenides and Heraclitus, or as the idea, the essence, the intuition of the soul of the pure essences—all these have a very particular background in the revelatory experiences of the Greeks. Here we come to the concept of reason, and I would say there is a real conflict here between Niebuhr and myself. He devaluates reason and I still stick to the classical concept of reason as *logos* in the universal sense.

Question (Professor Liston Pope): Professor Tillich, I once went with Richard Niebuhr to hear Reinhold Niebuhr speak. I suppose I should not quote Richard in his absence. But I am sure he has said this to Reinhold many times. I turned to him and said, "What did you think of the lecture?" And he said, "I don't see how Reinie talks so much about sin without talking more about grace." You didn't say very much today about Niebuhr's view of grace. Do you think he has developed that side of his theology adequately, or do you think he will be remembered primarily as a critic and analyst of sin?

Professor Tillich: I feel that the impact he has made on the whole situation did not come from his doctrine of grace, which is the Protestant doctrine of Justification with some elements of Catholic substantial thinking. I think we need this absolutely in Protestantism. For this reason I agree with him, but I don't think that this side of him—you see he also spoke about everything in spite of Bill Pauck. When somebody says, Why don't you talk more about and so and so? then I often said, "I did." But that doesn't help. The impact which one makes is usually determined not only by what one does, but also the situation in which the listeners are; and the situation in this country was such that whatever he would have said about grace would not have made the tremendous impact which his analysis of the human situation has made. And, therefore, I believe that we must simply accept—and this is also a criticism of the system. Here I agree with you that the system helps us only—has helped me always—to discover the relationships of ideas. But the system as it is finally elaborated has a limited effect. Those elements in the system which have been written with the lifeblood of the author, but not with the logical consistency with which he draws the lines from one thought to the other, have the greatest effect. I could show this in all great systems, which always—as you rightly say—speak about everything. They have to do so in order to show the consistency of their thinking. If they don't do it, the students come and say, You said something inconsistent; and then the systematician is completely lost. Therefore, this must be done. But when it is done, the impact—and I am so glad that you ask this question—is conditioned by the *kairos*. This is as much valid of Niebuhr as of any of those philosophers of the past who had their impact not with the whole of their system but with that which was *en kairo*. And if somebody was *en kairo* then it was Niebuhr in the thirties of this century.

PAUL TILLICH

Question (Dr. John MacKay): I wanted to express what for me has been the chief concern and problem in Niebuhr's thought. It is ontological in character and it appears to me to be the problem which contemporary theology tends to avoid. I refer to the question of what St. Paul might call "the new man in Christ." The question I would raise is, does the Christian man or the "new man" constitute a unique ontological reality? I might say that way back in the early thirties I used to discuss this with Barth as he was when he came to Bonn and I came to know him first. I feel that he has tended to change in his conception and to attach more reality to Christian experience and the ontological reality of "the new man in Christ." I would ask you, sir, whether you feel that Niebuhr considers that there is an ontological reality in the "new man" in the classical, Biblical, Christian sense that crosses the boundaries of Roman Catholicism, Protestantism, and Eastern Orthodoxy, and what your own view is of that ontological reality as differing from those who are involved simply in the human situation?

Professor Tillich: It's very difficult to combine the concept of new being to which you, as I understand you, John, refer in connection with the two concepts *essential* and *existential being*. The new being is new insofar as it cannot be derived from the two others; their disruptedness, the conflict between essence and existence puts the question, but the answer cannot be derived from them. You can only say that the new being is the ultimate possibility of creaturely being, but a possibility which is only a possibility if the eternal new being, which is also the old being, implies both essence and existence and transcends them, and appears in time and space. I think, in this point, I would completely agree with Niebuhr. But there is some other thing and here I really don't know. When I read, for instance, his interpretation of the Paulinian word, *yet not I, but Christ liveth in me* (Gal. 2:20), in *The Nature and Destiny of Man* (II, 4), he shows there with great dialectical skill the highly dialectical situation. And he does that in all his sermons. I know that many people have criticized his sermons just for this reason—that he never comes down to the new being. But in the moment in which it is outspoken, then already the question mark of the Protestant Principle is put behind it. And I must confess that something like this has also happened to me. In this respect, we are in the same boat. Here he is equally influenced by Luther's continuous paradoxical statement about *simul justus, simul peccator*. So that people who want to come for a moment at least to rest in a quieting Christian experience—even for a moment—immediately feel the thorn of his sermon, or his interpretation, in their spirit (which he calls flesh), namely, a spirit which wants to rest. I would never dare to criticize him on this point, but here I would say, Where do I get more help? Where can we find this kind of restful acceptance—as the Biblical men and the Reformers often expressed it, even Luther sometimes, but only in ecstatic moments—Where can we find this when we have this radical dialectics of ego and non-ego, but in Christ? I don't know how far Niebuhr was also influenced on this point by the saying of the Barthian school: Even the Divine Spirit, who in Christian tradition is that which is us working in us, cannot be experienced so that we can say, "I have it." We can only say, "I believe that I believe. I have the faith that I have faith." But we can never say directly, "I have faith," or "I have the Spirit." Now here we are on a point where the dialectics almost never come down to earth. And if I understand you rightly, then you have expressed in this moment a criticism which is against my own theological structure, but out of which I don't know the way, in view of the realism about the human predicament which I share with Niebuhr.

JOHN C. BENNETT:

*Reinhold Niebuhr's Contribution
to Christian Social Ethics*

JOHN C. BENNETT:

Reinhold Niebuhr's significance as a thinker is the greater because he has done so much more than think. Not only has he been ceaselessly active in public affairs, but also he has always been available to people of all kinds. For decades he has been in his office at Union Seminary, unprotected by anyone, and ready to talk with the people who came to his open door, a steady procession of students, statesmen, churchmen, professors, and cranks. During the thirties and the forties he must have founded or joined at least a hundred organizations. Some of these were political organizations such as the Liberal Party in New York and Americans for Democratic Action. Some were journals. He was the founder of *The World Tomorrow*. He has been the Editor of *Christianity and Crisis*, and of *Radical Religion*, which changed its name to *Christianity and Society*. Many of his organizations were created to defend groups or individuals needing defenders—labor groups until they acquired means of self-defense, Negroes, sharecroppers, Jews, Germans who were victims of unconditional surrender.

We cannot understand his thought unless we realize

this openness to the world, this activity based upon his sense of justice and his amazing generosity. Paul Tillich has described himself as living on the boundary of contrasting worlds and interests, and in this respect he and Reinhold Niebuhr have much in common. Perhaps one difference is that Niebuhr has been more polemical across some of these boundaries and has not absorbed so many elements into his system of thought. And yet Niebuhr, after excoriating the illusions of many a liberal rationalist, will be found the next day sitting with these victims of illusion on a committee drafting a political manifesto or planning to rescue someone, perhaps some poor Utopian, from jail.

Reinhold Niebuhr is catalogued as a theologian more than anything else and he has done more than any other American to change the climate of theology. He likes to say that he is not a theologian, meaning that he is not the kind of academic specialist whom he often admires and even at times envies, and yet I think we can say that he is the kind of theologian who gives the academic specialist something to write about. Theology would indeed be a dreary occupation if it became the study of academic specialists by academic specialists. The great theologians have often been makers of history even in their own time. It may be a symbol of what I am saying that while he never wrote a Ph.D. thesis, there are few living persons about whom so many Ph.D. theses are written. Another remarkable aspect of Niebuhr's role among scholars is that he has been a formative influence on a diverse group of scholars and practitioners in the field of international relations, and yet he has never been a specialist here. His many writings on this subject, except for one book written a few years ago, have been articles and editorials. One subject of interest to the academic specialists in international relations is the influence of Reinhold Niebuhr on the thought in their field.

There is another whole dimension of his activity and influence—his preaching and his work as a Christian apologist, if you will accept this word in its best sense. His preaching in colleges and universities for four decades has been one of the factors in his very pervasive influence. Students and professors who usually stayed away from chapel would flock to hear him. Also in this he and Paul Tillich have had the same experience. There are those who say that his sermons are all on one subject, the relation of sin and grace. But there is always something unique and unforgettable in each sermon, in his use of the text and its Biblical context. There are always new illustrations of sin, and sin is always combined in a different way with the finiteness, the tragedy, the irony, and also the goodness and the greatness of our existence; and as the years have passed, there has been more about grace. Theologians on the European continent have argued for many years as to whether or not there can be an apologetic for Christianity. But while they have argued, Reinhold Niebuhr has acted as an apologist by showing the relevance of the Christian revelation for the hard problems of our history. He has convinced many of our contemporaries that the Christian diagnosis of the human situation is essentially true and he has drawn some of these into the circle of those who feel claimed by the Christian Gospel. But always he has been able to present both aspects of the Christian faith in such a way as to make them more meaningful to our contemporaries who are fearful of obscurantism and false piety.

I shall say something now about Niebuhr's method of thinking. There are few places where Niebuhr avows any method. Paul Tillich once said: "Niebuhr does not ask, 'How can I know?' He starts knowing." So it is with his method of thought; we have to watch it as he starts thinking. There is a living dialectic in his thought which seems to grow naturally out of polemics. He is often much clearer in showing what is wrong with many positions than he is in giving content to his own position; or rather, we often have to infer this content from his criticisms of those who are in conflict with each other. His books often have this structure of polemics around the compass. He shows what is wrong with Catholicism, Calvinism, Lutheranism, Protestant sectarianism, theological liberalism, Marxism, secular rationalism, and so forth. There is often a shift of emphasis here from decade to decade depending on what kind of error is the greatest threat to his truth. His early polemics against liberal optimism, against doctrines of progress, were quite successful. With the help of Hitler and Stalin and many events he won his battles against these positions.

In the course of his polemics he gave aid and comfort to what is often called "Neo-orthodoxy," and now he finds this very repellent and often he sounds more like a liberal again. I think it should be said that at no point did he ever have any kind of theological authoritarianism in him. Only those who had no real understanding of him bracketed him with orthodoxy, Biblicism, irrationalism. He has always been critical of rationalistic schemes of meaning, but this has been in the interests of a broad empiricism by which he kept himself open to the realities neglected by such schemes. Perhaps one source of confusion is that he has been a master in presenting rhetorical or homiletical paradoxes which have been ways of underlining a point. This is quite different from a reckless positing of paradoxes as descriptive of reality. He does accept a few such paradoxes that continually reappear in Christian history and that still remain after decades of his own critical thought as inescapable for his own mind. But this kind of paradox, such as is to be seen in the relations of grace and freedom, is not projected by an irrationalist tendency in his thought but is accepted because of his openness to the complexities of experience. I do not say that he may not have been carried away at times by his own rhetorical paradoxes, but usually it is other people who are confused by them and attribute to him an excessive use of paradox in the substance of his thought.

I shall now deal briefly with two aspects of this thought which can give us understanding of his contribution to Christian ethics and to the presuppositions and goals and criteria for social policy within the nation. Niebuhr is basically a theologian who sees the implications of his theology for Christian ethics, but he has never addressed himself primarily to the Church as Church. He has always emphasized the need for the Church to think and speak about the great issues confronting society, and I doubt if we can make a very clear distinction between

JOHN C. BENNETT

the substance of what he says explicitly as a theologian and churchman, and what he says when he speaks to the public. But this is a problem raised by Niebuhr's thought that does need careful examination. The two subjects that I shall discuss are the following: (1) his doctrine of man and its implications for ethics; (2) his way of uniting absolute ethical perspectives with pragmatic methods.

The Doctrine of Man

It was Niebuhr's rediscovery of neglected elements in the classical Christian understanding of man that made the most decisive impression on the contemporary mind both in the Church and in the world. Often it almost seems that he is blamed for the origin of sin because he rediscovered some dimensions of it. Journalistically, he has been widely presented as the great pessimist, as the one who has deflated man in the interests of an orthodox doctrine of original sin.

His thought has been in continuous movement even in this area of doctrine that is so central to it. It was first expressed in terms of his polemics against rationalistic optimism, liberal idealism, and all forms of what he calls utopianism. But as his thought matured during the thirties when he was writing his greatest book, *The Nature and Destiny of Man,* his doctrine of man could be seen in the context of a total theology of man in relation to the judgmen and to the grace of God. Always in his more mature writings sin is seen as the other side of man's greatness and of man's promise. Sin is the corruption of freedom which is itself a mark of man's greatness. Man's self-transcendence which is the mark of the image of God in him is also the source of man's capacity for prideful imperialisms, for the endlessly destructive evils which cause his greatest dreams and achievements to turn sour. Niebuhr is never weary of saying that it is the pretentious idealism or utopianism in human movements which often makes them most intolerable.

Niebuhr is more vivid, more precise, and more elaborate in his setting forth of the sin of man than he is in what he has to say about redemption. And yet always one can see that the antidote for sin is for man to see himself as he is, without illusions, in his finiteness under God, before whom alone his finiteness can be recognized. And the ultimate anxieties which drive men to express ever more destructively their sinful self-centeredness and pride can only be overcome as they see themselves by faith under the forgiveness of God. This forgiveness is revealed most fully on the cross of Christ, but God who is revealed in Christ is known in his saving work apart from Christ. Indeed, we may say that Niebuhr—and this is another point in common between him and Tillich—is a theologian who greatly stresses common grace, grace that is mediated apart from a conscious relationship with Christ. He is an enemy of the theological or ecclesiastical monopolist, but for him the ultimate criterion of all revelations and mediations of God is Christ. His attitude toward the conversion of the Jews, which has been much publicized, illustrates this position.

I can give some idea of the range and complexity of Niebuhr's doctrine of man if I put before you three statements about it.

JOHN C. BENNETT

1. The first is that man's sinful pride and egocentricity is to be found on every level of personal development, of social or cultural advance, of religious pretension. This is probably Niebuhr's major warning to Church and culture, to those who are guardians of a *status quo* of which they are proud, and to those who engage in revolution to establish a new order. There is no spot where we are not vulnerable to the temptation to abuse power or to organize the good in our achievements in terms of a limited interest. Indeed, the higher the advance the more subtle but often the more destructive the sin. He turns this criticism against the history of the Church, and I think there is no passage in all of his writings that reveals more clearly his main concern on the negative side than this passage: "The sad experiences of Christian history show how human pride and spiritual arrogance rise to new heights precisely at the point where the claims of sanctity are made without due qualification."[1]

I have often quoted that passage, but I never until this lecture added this comment: please note that the claims of sanctity may have some status if there are "due qualifications."

2. The second statement is that Niebuhr is in no sense a dogmatic pessimist or fatalist. He retains a higher and more hopeful view of man's possibilities in part because he has not sought to buttress this view with illusions which history easily refutes. One of his favorite phrases is "indeterminate possibilities." A sentence that expresses this side of his thought is the following: "There are no limits to be set in history for the achievement of more universal

brotherhood, for the development of more perfect and more inclusive human relations."[2] He will be quick to point out ways in which societies project particular schemes of hope that do transcend limits, but this is chiefly because there are inherent in them either pretensions which generate their own poisons or a lack of prudence in relation to the conditions of human life which cannot be transcended if they are not recognized or astutely beguiled, as he often says. This statement should not suggest to anyone unlimited cumulative progress. There will always be temptations and threats on the new levels of advance and always the danger of retrogression, but what is involved here is a guard against the kind of dogmatic pessimism that refuses to deal with particular problems with a hopeful openness.

3. The third statement is that Niebuhr warns against a perverse complacency that sometimes develops when Christians become impressed by the sinful limitations upon all human achievement. Paul must have encountered it when he exclaimed: "What then? Are we to sin because we are not under law but under grace? By no means!" Niebuhr echoes Paul when he writes: "Thus the saints are tempted to continue to sin that grace may abound, while the sinners toil and sweat to make human relations a little more tolerable and slightly more just."[3] This appreciation of the "sinners," of persons who have no traditional piety to cushion their consciences but who are moved by a passion for justice and do the best they can, is a persistent theme in Niebuhr's writings and conversation. The pious of the liberal sort who mix their piety with idealistic illu-

sions, and the pious of the orthodox sort who allow the gospel of forgiveness to make them prematurely complacent about what they cannot do because of sin, come in equally for condemnation. One of the sharpest of his comments of this sort is his criticism of Brunner's illustration of the judge who, because of his faith in justification by faith, is sustained religiously when he pronounces a sentence which, while according to the law, is in his own mind unjust because the law is unjust. I do not think that Niebuhr is quite fair to Brunner's use of the illustration but his condemnation of it reveals much about his own thought. He writes: "Fortunately there have always been judges who have never heard of this doctrine of justification by faith and who have, therefore, been prompted by a sensitive conscience to apply the law as justly as possible."[4] I doubt if one could find a better illustration of Niebuhr's openness to those who are outside the Christian circle and of his contempt for all the false uses of the cushions of piety.

Those three statements which I have just presented about the same general question: "What are the limits of moral achievement because of man's sin?" are given to illustrate a method of thinking. Each statement qualifies the others. It would be impossible to draw from them anything like a precise calculus concerning what is possible. Rather we have powerful warnings against three different errors, and the one to be emphasized at any given time depends upon which error is most tempting. The warning that has had the most influence, that has given Niebuhr his distinctive place in modern Christian thought and political theory, is the warning against the illusions of the idealist and the utopian; the soft idealist or utopian who believes that the cruel realities of history can be transformed by loving persuasion, and the hard idealist or utopian who by force will impose his ideals upon the world and mercilessly sacrifice concrete people for a future goal.

Perhaps the most important consequence of Niebuhr's doctrine of man for social ethics and for policy is his insistence in all areas on the balancing of power. In all situations power must be kept in check, and this cannot be done merely by legal structures; it depends upon an equilibrium of social forces. This should not be static and it need not involve overt violence. Also, the healthier the society the more the nations, classes, or other social forces that balance each other will all participate in common loyalties or common interests which prevent the conflict between them from becoming absolute. He has great appreciation for the traditions and habits of mutual respect which have developed in some cultures, especially in the British culture. In the relations between nations the common loyalties and interests are minimal, but he has continually expressed the hope that the common interest in survival may still be a bond even between the United States and the Soviet Union.

His rejection of pacifism is essentially a form of this emphasis upon the need of raising up effective power to counter any center of power that threatens to be tyrannical. In the 1930's he came to accept moral responsibility for the military resistance against National Socialism. Sinful and fallible nations had to be the instruments of this resistance, and yet this did not for him annul their claim to moral support. Christian responsibility for justice for the neighbor threatened by a power as evil as that of the Nazis involved participation in the use of national power. Pacifists who believed that they escaped the guilt of history were in his mind misguided because they contributed indirectly to the triumph of oppressive forces. It was his Christian realism about man that caused him to insist on the necessity of accepting the reality of power and of finding ways of using power that would serve justice. Always he has sought to prevent conflicts of power from becoming brutal and violent. But he has refused to absolutize nonviolent forms of resistance as universally to be preferred.

The theological and ethical foundation of this emphasis on the balance of power is well presented in the following passage:

Justification by faith in the realm of justice means that we will not regard the pressures and counterpressures, the tensions, the overt and covert conflicts by which justice is achieved and maintained as normative in the absolute sense; but neither will we ease our conscience by seeking to escape from involvement in them. We will know that we cannot purge ourselves of the sin and guilt in which we are involved by the moral ambiguities of politics without also disavowing responsibility for the creative possibilities of justice.

His interpretation of the case for democracy is closely related to this emphasis upon the need of balancing power in the nation. He says: "It is the highest achievement of democratic societies that they embody the principle of resistance to government within the principle of government itself."[6] The lawful use of political power by various groups within the nation and the check upon their use of it, the preservation of openness and pluralism with all of the civil liberties that enable those who are injured to protest—these ways and structures of democracy can best be defended in terms of his doctrine of man. It is most important to see how both the positive and the negative poles of this doctrine are involved. Dogmatic pessimists or cynics have no case for democracy. They are likely to put all their emphasis upon the preservation of order and to fear change as likely to be for the worse, and especially to fear the extension of power to the people as a whole whom they distrust. Niebuhr often refers to Martin Luther and Thomas Hobbes in this connection and sees their pessimism as related to their support of despotism. One of the most famous sentences that Niebuhr ever wrote is the one in which he emphasizes the two sides of democracy: "Man's capacity for justice makes democracy possible; but man's inclination to injustice makes democracy necessary."[7] Those words give us very well the political consequence of Niebuhr's doctrine of man.

The Normative and the Pragmatic

The second major theme that I shall discuss is the relationship between the Christian norm, general social values, and pragmatic calculation in Niebuhr's thought.

It is sometimes said that Niebuhr's thought is so pragmatic that it moves along realistically with the trends of history without sufficient control by permanent ethical norms. Exposure to what Niebuhr says about one subject, especially in a journalistic context, can easily lead to that impression but I think that it is quite inaccurate. The pragmatism in Niebuhr's thought comes from his fear of allowing any particular value or principle or law from becoming absolute in itself and yielding a series of consequences for unforeseen situations by means of a system of casuistry. Instead he emphasizes love as the only absolute, and then relates love to concrete situations by means of several values which need to be kept in balance dynamically. The exact nature of this balance will change with the circumstances. He is not a very systematic writer, and there are often shades of difference when he returns from time to time to the same subject.

There has been a tendency in his thought from his earliest writings to describe love as the pinnacle of ethics which is so pure that it is hard to see how it can be related to anything else. Out of this preoccupation with pure sacrificial love which is revealed in the Cross of Christ there has developed the formula of love as an "impossible possibility." There is a strong perfectionist impulse in Niebuhr's thought which calls for a conscious check to keep him from becoming irrelevant. His fierce arguments against pacifism often seem to be arguments against a position which on its perfectionist side tempts him. In terms of social ethics and politics he is always uncompromising, but religiously he settles for a compromise when he welcomes the testimony of the Mennonite type of pacifism, which has no political illusions and yet remains a corrective for the spirit of those involved in the ambiguities of history.

He relates this pure love to the mutual love which is possible among us by saying that such love "can only be initiated by a type of disinterestedness which dispenses with historical justification."[8] Mutual love is not a matter of egocentric calculation on both sides; but if it is love at all, the impulse of *agape* is in it, and each will sacrifice for the other, and neither will withhold love as a bargaining point if it is not reciprocated. He says: "The grace of sacrificial love prevents mutual love from degenerating into a mere calculation of mutual advantages."[9]

The relation of love to justice is a theme that brings us close to the heart of his ethics. Justice is one extension of mutual love. As he puts it:

Systems and principles of justice are the servants and instruments of the spirit of brotherhood in so far as they extend the sense of obligation towards the other, (a) from an immediately felt obligation, prompted by obvious need, to a continued obligation expressed in fixed principles of mutual support; (b) from a simple relation of the self and one 'other' to the complex relations of the self and the 'others'; and (c) finally from the obligations which the community defines from its more impartial perspective.[10]

Indeed, the perfect love that he often describes as belonging to a pinnacle that transcends all of these considerations of justice would, I believe, in the light of Niebuhr's thought as a whole be less perfect than a love that relates itself to the problems and structures of justice. There is at this point in Niebuhr's thought both a problem of terminology and, more deeply, a meeting of two impulses that never at any level are clearly related to each other—the impulse guided by a pure heedless *agape* and the impulse guided by a loving sense of responsibility for the effect of what we do upon all men.

Niebuhr's central position can be seen by the way in which he contrasts his thought with other views of the relationship of love and justice. He repudiates the tendency which he finds in Luther to separate the two realms in which love and justice are realized. There is such a Lutheran separation, and there are passages in Luther which support it; but Niebuhr is attacked by many interpreters of Luther, not least by his colleague Wilhelm Pauck, for attributing this to Luther in a one-sided way. But as far as I can see, there is much that is slippery here. Niebuhr emphasizes an interaction between the two realms which one would scarcely learn from Luther, even though defenders of Luther may be right in saying that this is possible for Luther. If I may intervene in the debate about Luther, it seems to me that Niebuhr is clearly right at one point: Luther was not interested in the development of checks upon political power in the interests of justice. He had no more illusions than Niebuhr about princes, whom he expected to be either fools or knaves, but he could use them against the Pope, and he feared anarchy created by the peasants more than he feared injustice imposed by the prince. Niebuhr attacks Brunner who separates love and justice more clearly than Luther, though even this is a slippery matter, for when I asked Brunner about it, he volunteered the formula: "Justice is institutionalized love." That may go too far the other way.

Niebuhr rejects the idea that love can take the place of justice, if those who love only become more loving. No, there must be structures of justice to enable people to defend themselves against the loving who are so sure that they know best what is good for others. There are none so good that they can be entrusted with unchecked power over others, for there are too many illusions in any paternalistic love and also too much unacknowledged self-interest. Niebuhr is an expert on the forms of self-interest within the communities which are informed by love—especially family and church and the best academic communities.

Justice for Niebuhr is governed by the idea of equality. Not that he projects rationalistic schemes that make no distinctions between the needs and contributions and functions of people. Equality in that sense has no place in his thought. But equality for him is a principle of criticism that shows up the ideological taint, the corruption by the self-interest of the powerful, in all actual structures of justice. Perhaps the best illustration of this is his criticism of all forms of male domination in church and society. This criticism does not imply that there are no differences of role between men and women, but it does indicate that the kinds of inequality between men and women that exist come from the imperialism of men in the world and in the church, not least of priests in the church.

The transforming of the structures of justice so that they do embody greater equality comes both from love and from the struggles of the victims of injustice. I do not need to repeat what I have said about balancing of power here; my interest at the moment is to stress the point that love does seek to raise the structures of justice in the interests of the weak and the exploited.

The Role of Natural Law

I began this phase of the discussion with a reference to the problem of moral norms in relation to pragmatic ways of thinking about policy. I want to say something here about the much debated question of the role of "natural law." Niebuhr has a perpetual battle on two fronts—on the one side against Catholic stereotypes of natural law, and on the other side against the moral relativists, especially when they are Protestant theologians. His arguments with the Catholics have been carried on for many decades down to his latest article about the encyclical of John XXIII. He sees the Catholic system of natural law as much distorted by a tendency to absolutize the institutions of the Middle Ages and by what is for him an outrageous development of particular laws apart from love in such areas as sex and medicine. Niebuhr does not write many pages on this subject in these days without mentioning Catholic teaching about birth control as an example of the wrong use of natural law. On the other hand, he finds a great deal of wisdom in the teachings of the Catholic Church on many social and economic questions which he contrasts with the nineteenth-century ideology of the dominant Protestant individualism. He does not reject the belief that there is a moral wisdom that does not depend wholly on revelation. He continually emphasizes what Christians have in common with secularists who have a passion for justice and who combine dedication to the public welfare with great astuteness concerning policy.

When Niebuhr thinks about Karl Barth's strictures against natural law, he reacts with equal sharpness: "Karl Barth's belief that the moral life of man would possess no valid principles of guidance, if the Ten Commandments had not introduced such principles by revelation, is as absurd as it is unscriptural."[11] There is more to Barth than this, for Barth curiously enough shares Niebuhr's openness to those outside the Church and the circle of revelation. Yet that sentence does show clearly that Niebuhr has no patience with complete moral relativism whether or not it is found in a theological garment. There is great scope for relativism so far as concrete decisions are concerned, but those who make these decisions should be moved by love for the neighbor and what they decide to do should be seen under the ultimate judgment of love. More than that: love is related to the concrete decision by means of the order and the justice and the freedom that are good for the neighbor, for all neighbors. The relativism of the concrete decision is really the effect of relating to each other these permanent criteria and of relating all of them to the contingent and quite unpredictable circumstances which call for action. This is quite different from a deductive casuistry that knows most of the answers in advance, even about a code for air-raid shelters, and it is quite different from an absolute moral idealism that seeks to impose a law of nonviolence or the claims of democratic forms upon all situations; but it is not an unguided relativism or a pragmatism without norms.

One of the most significant developments in Niebuhr's thought from the 1930's to the 1950's, closely related to the pragmatic method of much of his thought, was his movement away from a dogmatic socialism which was controlled to a considerable extent by the Marxist conception of history. This dogmatic socialism caused him to be almost contemptuous of the New Deal reforms until the late thirties. His confidence in socialism as a total structure dissolved very gradually. There was a basis for this in his doctrine of man, which prepared him to see the dangerous illusions in Marxist expectations, both in the context of communism and in the context of the democratic socialism that continued to guide his thought about economic life into the 1940's. The clarification of his doctrine of man at this point, the shock from Stalinism, the later attraction of the New Deal revolution and all that it symbolized, and preoccupation with international political problems—all of these factors were present in his movement away from socialism as a system. The time came when he began to speak of Burke with more respect than of Marx. Yet American conservatives should not take comfort from this. There is no more effective critic of American conservatism based upon individualism and the primacy of the business man. One of his favorite adjectives is "stupid," and there is continuity from his days in Detroit until now in his use of this adjective to describe the representatives of this American conservative ideology. I doubt if his place in the American political spectrum has changed in two decades. He finds more wisdom in British conservatism than in American conservatism, but he will always be more open than any who think of themselves as conservatives to the claims of justice for the people who are neglected or exploited wherever they may be.

It would be satisfying to me to conclude this address with words of eulogy for Reinhold Niebuhr, but I can surely take that for granted. It is more fitting, in view of the continuous movement in his thought, to mention briefly several unsolved problems which his thought poses for us and for him.

Perhaps the deepest problem is what is to be said to a generation that has never shared the optimistic illusions over which Niebuhr won so many victories. In the distinctive theological dimension of this problem, Niebuhr has recognized that his thought should make more room than is evident in his major books for the possibilities of real change as a gift of grace in the Christian life; for something more than his old formula, "change in principle but not in fact," suggests. He has discarded that formula. I am thinking of more than this theological dimension within the Church when I say that the very success of Niebuhr's polemics leaves a need for hope and morale for people more tempted by despair than by false optimism.

Second, I think that the movement of his thought away from economic problems because of his preoccupation with political problems leaves almost an empty space which needs to be filled by thinkers who share his basic outlook. This is true especially in the many new countries where social and economic revolution for the sake of justice is a primary concern.

Third, there is always the danger that those who take from Niebuhr's thought only his political realism will develop an ethic that is little more than a reflection of the exigencies of Western strategy in the cold war. There are in Niebuhr's theology correctives for this tendency as well as for idealistic illusions, and these need to be heard. He has not directed his polemics very strongly against the illusions of political realism but there are pointers toward them in his many brief discussions of what he calls "the nuclear dilemma." He has lost his earlier Churchillian confidence in the security provided by the balance of terror. Recently he has said: "Ultimately, the ever-accelerated pace of the arms race must lead to disaster, even if neither side consciously desires the ultimate war."[12] He has at various times said that if we ever use the nuclear weapons, "we will annihilate ourselves not only physically but morally." In a published conversation he shows his sense of the depths of the nuclear dilemma beyond those that are usually discussed. He said: "If the bomb were ever used, I would hope it would kill me, because the moral situation would be something that I could not contemplate." Notice how different that is from the common idea that one would rather die than face the miseries of the situation. And yet Niebuhr went on to say: "At the same time you cannot disavow its use absolutely prematurely without bowing yourself out of responsibility for the whole generation."[13] In a discussion of the possibility of initiating the nuclear stage of a war over Berlin, Niebuhr says that the speculations about the consequences of a nuclear catastrophe have omitted a consideration of "the moral consequences of initiating the dread conflict." He asks: "Could a civilization loaded with this monstrous guilt have enough moral health to survive?"[14]

Niebuhr has helped us to grasp the religious dimension of this nuclear dilemma as it comes to us as a matter of fate. One of his favorite texts from St. Paul expresses this ultimate dimension of faith: "If we live, we live to the Lord, and if we die, we die to the Lord; so then, whether we live or whether we die, we are the Lord's." (Rom. 14:8) The question remains: how far will there be an area of moral freedom as we confront this dilemma in the next decade? What ethical thinking should guide the political choice between military strategies? This is an area in which Reinhold Niebuhr's thought is needed because his realism remains under the criticism of love and he has the habit of recognizing new illusions as well as old.

DISCUSSION:

Question (Henry Smith Leiper): A very minor question. I tried to remember anything that Niebuhr ever wrote that I happened to read that reflected this horror of initiating the use of the bomb in the face of the fact that we did it. All the world knows that and we seem to forget it.

Professor Bennett: He signed the Calhoun report which renounced that. This is one of the problems of fate that we have today that this was done. It happened then without much discussion because nobody knew about it.

Question (Professor Wilhelm Pauck): I've often wondered about Niebuhr's ecclesiology, churchmanship, not in the practical sense—you've made several remarks about it— but more in the theological sense. He's never denied his origins in the Evangelical Synod. He's a minister of the Evangelical Reformed Church, now the United Church, but he has never emphasized it. [*Professor Bennett:* He and Paul Tillich are in the same church now.] Yes, in the same church, and Tillich is more or less in the same boat in this respect. Professor Tillich has an articulate ecclesiology.

Professor Bennett: Of course, how is it related to concrete churches? You have to argue that.

Professor Pauck: But now Niebuhr speaks as a Christian, a very pragmatic Christian, and as a Protestant. But what his relation to the institutions of Protestantism, the ecclesiastical structure and the ecclesiastical procedures, is doesn't become plain, although he attacks, as you have said, ecclesiastical monopolists and all the pretensions of churchmen and priests, and is always out for the hypocrites of all sorts. But what his own sense of the church is is barely intimated, or am I wrong there?

Professor Bennett: I think that's right. But he does have, of course, a great liturgical sense. I suppose his liturgical writings will be published sometime and this will give a somewhat different picture of Niebuhr. He thinks of the Church as the community of grace; as the bearer of the revelation in a very real sense. But the moment he thinks of the Church as a corporate body that makes claims for itself, then he is on another tack. He doesn't want that very much. He never makes claims for the Church as a corporate body. But I think he does think of the Church as a community in which the Word is preached, and which does actually mediate grace to people. But his fear of ecclesiastical doctrines is a good deal like his fear of doctrines of sanctification. He is always talking about the Catholic heresies whenever the Church is emphasized very much as a matter of claim. Wouldn't that be true?

Professor Pauck: Yes, I think you are right. It's a strangely spiritual conception of the Church.

JOHN C. BENNETT

Professor Bennett: Yes, but its activity is not of that sort at all.

Professor Pauck: Yes, but there is a certain conflict there.

Professor Bennett: Yes, I think this is true. Most of the critics of Niebuhr, whenever they write criticism, generally say he doesn't have a doctrine of the Church. That's usually what they say.

Question (Professor Taubes): I would like you to help me on a point that always baffles me in reading Niebuhr. The disillusionment with Utopia I got from a man who I think equals Niebuhr in strength—Max Weber. He made a differentiation between ethics of conscience and ethics of responsibility and worked it out in a way that I think can stand up to any of the other critics of Utopianism. So far so right. Then I came to America and began to read Niebuhr, and saw it was the same path of Max Weber, except for one difference. He calls this Christian realism. Now Max Weber never dreamt to consider that Christian, because he could get it equally out of Machiavelli or the ancients. You don't need a Christian dispensation to find that out. It baffles me that Niebuhr makes so great a thing of that. If this would be all that we learn from him, I think it would be a lesson not at all necessary to divide the ages between B.C. and A.D.

Professor Bennett: I think there are two things I would say about that. One is that much of the content of this realism is a matter of common sense, or hard experience, and can be seen from many points of view; but in the case of Christian realism, particularly in the understanding of the depth of the person, there seems to me to be a more penetrating understanding of the person's selfhood in relation to this. Niebuhr finds this much more in Paul than anywhere else. But secondly, this Christian realism is never cynicism, never Machiavellianism. It's never purely a negative approach. It's always seen in relationship to the image of God in man, and the very source of the problem is man's self-transcendence and freedom which are marks of the image of God. So it is keeping together the dignity of man and the sin of man that makes Niebuhr quite different from any of the secular realists. Wouldn't you think that's true?

Professor Taubes: In the consequences it didn't quite come out.

Professor Bennett: Well, sometimes in the consequences it doesn't. You get people who learn only the negative side of the realism because that's the more obvious—the diagnosis. That's quite true. Niebuhr used to say often that the Harvard orthodoxy was to accept the Christian analysis of the human situation without the Gospel.

Professor Taubes: That's something I sometimes feel in him too.

Professor Bennett: Well, that's only because you see him in certain contexts.

Question (Dr. Hutchison): Might it not be argued that Niebuhr's social ethic is a corollary of assumptions which he's never taken the time fully to state, but which are essentially Christian and traditionally so. What he has spent his life doing is to draw out certain pertinent corollaries.

Professor Bennett: I think that's true, yes. Yes, he has never had a systematic methodology at all.

Professor Taubes: I understand that, but it struck me that in his critique of Utopianism he succeeded marvelously with the help of Hitler and Stalin. It may be that there is a sort of Utopianism in Christianity which is worthwhile preserving in spite of all this criticism.

Professor Bennett: In a certain way he does preserve this as a source of criticism, but he's embarrassed about it, because he still has this perfectionism in his own basic attitude. But actually, isn't one of the reasons Niebuhr gets somewhat caricatured, that it is this negative realism which people can fasten on journalistically and gets played up in *Time* magazine, and everybody reads and understands what it is about; whereas the other things involved aren't easily seen.

Question (Dr. Moran Weston): Professor Bennett, would you say that Niebuhr has any picture of society now that is either feasible or acceptable?

Professor Bennett: He certainly doesn't have any final picture of society. I think society for him always involves dealing with proximate problems, trying to improve situations a little bit with this balancing of forces and also with the Christian grace too. He doesn't plan much about the Christian grace—I agree with comments there—but he presupposes it to some extent. You get his recent article about the new nations which have trouble getting democratic societies and democratic structures, and he almost resigns himself to this. They will not be democracies. They will not represent any kind of pattern that we would want to universalize. But he hopes they will not be just tyrannies; that there will be some openness in them.

Dr. Weston: What will help man to avoid the intiative in the use of the atomic bomb for example?

Professor Bennett: Well, I think his present thinking is—just as Doctor Tillich said the other night over the television—that if at some point in the immediate Berlin situation we were in danger of defeat, he would not prevent defeat by initiating a nuclear exchange, which would be an indefinite thing in its effect—an unlimited thing. It's different from Hiroshima: because of the fact that we had a monopoly, we did it, and that was the end. This would be endless—might be. I wouldn't want to stress this too much because he hasn't developed this. This is just a hint he has thrown out, because he is as much puzzled as anyone else is. And he would be the first to say that a person making policy is not going to announce this.

Professor Bennett (with reference to the untaped comment of Father John LaFarge): Father LaFarge was saying that there is no dynamism in this piece-by-piece approach, just fixing up things a little bit here, pushing a little bit there, preserving the best balance that you can, and I think that's quite true. And this is one of the places where I suppose his thought would have to be supplemented. There would have to be something more than that actually—some vision of something more than that. But at the same time, the policy makers would have to take this pretty seriously as the way things are. Wouldn't they?

Father LaFarge: We need a vision!

Professor Bennett: We need a vision. Well, you know the last paragraph in *Moral Man and Immoral Society,* which was published about 1932; the last paragraph emphasizes the need of dreams and visions here. He says he hopes that these will not be corrupted too soon; and then he lived a little while and he came to think these visions get corrupted too soon, and he put them aside. But now it isn't only that, but it's his prudence. If you have a vision that turns out to be irrelevant you'll do the wrong things too. It's not only a matter of the corruption of the vision, but it may not be quite relevant.

Question (Unidentified): Has Niebuhr withdrawn those definitions of an open society that he used to give us?

Professor Bennett: Oh, I imagine not. I think that open society would be the best dream, but then that's still rather negative—not negative exactly, but lacking positive content.

Question (Dr. Heimann): I've been wondering for quite awhile, and I should say increasingly so, particularly after coming back from Europe, that it never occurs to him, and I am afraid I have to say it never occurs to any of us, to say anything that people behind the Iron Curtain can use. The social-political views that we develop and discuss among us are for people in a free society. And that is the reason his influence the farther you go East is less and less. Our mutual friend Charlie West has drawn this comparison between Barth and him. He says Barth is a preacher in the church, and Niebuhr is a Christian in the world. The Christian in the world has quite a hard time; the preacher in the church has a very good time if there is nothing else but the church to cling to, as there is behind the Iron Curtain. There is really nothing in his teachings that could be used behind the Iron Curtain by the Christians there, be they Lutherans or Greek or whatever else. This is a grave omission—I may be wrong—a grave failure.

Professor Bennett: It's historically conditioned, I think. You remember that Charlie West in that book also says— he loves Niebuhr and he is more formed by Niebuhr than by anybody else—that Niebuhr is from some standpoints Hromadka in reverse to the people on the other side. He is simply the man who stands for American policy and Western strategy. I think he does transcend these. Therefore, what you say is true. He doesn't have anything to say to people that are living on the other side of the Iron Curtain. Also he doesn't have very much to say to people in Asia, partly because he doesn't have any interest. Paul Tillich knows how Niebuhr has a great way of talking about the non-historical religions: In one sentence they get dismissed very easily.

Doctor Heimann: This, I think, is the justification for the suspicion that he is most interested in the Cold War, and that all his teachings are really applicable to the Cold War and only on the one side and not on the other.

Professor Bennett: That's true. He has many disciples whom I know in Asia, but they always have to recognize that, while they can get something of his spirit and method, what he says isn't very relevant to Asian problems, problems of revolution in Asia now.

Question (Professor Tom Driver): In this connection, I've been thinking for a few minutes and I've been wondering about it before, as a matter of historical development in Niebuhr's thought, how much do you think that this kind of thing that Professor Heimann points to is the result of the actions which he took counter to the Nazi threat? I've often wondered if it wasn't one of the ironies of history that in making this stand Niebuhr did not commit himself more to the forms of Western capitalism and democracy than he would otherwise have liked to have done.

Professor Bennett: Niebuhr constantly says that we must not transfer to Communism the same strategies that we used in dealing with National Socialism. He makes a great deal of that difference. But I suppose that it is true that he was molded as a person who is primarily concerned with what government is doing, the United States Government, and you do have a certain historical conditioning here that is very real. I wish you would comment on that, Paul Tillich. What do you think about that point?

Professor Tillich: Yes, I have had the same feeling for a long time, and I remember that we sometimes talked about it. I was always glad that you modified to a certain extent in articles in *Christianity and Crisis* and elsewhere this one sided anti-Communist attitude.

Professor Bennett: Of course, the Niebuhr that one knows around the corridors and the elevator is always more qualified than the Niebuhr that writes publicly. He makes room for things that he doesn't actually say. That doesn't help the person who wants to understand him.

Question (Professor H. Searle Bates): Would you comment on this problem? Perhaps it might be in your list of continuing problems for Niebuhr in the close of his life. What about the need of this generation for practical norms in conduct and guiding lines in ethical standards as over against Niebuhr's continual onslaught against moralism?

Professor Bennett: That's a very interesting point. You know—those of you who know Union Seminary well—that for about twenty years—thirty years maybe now—Dr. Van Dusen and Dr. Niebuhr have preached at each other in the chapel, and usually on this question of moralism. The reason is that Dr. Van Dusen is concerned about the sins of the weak who need some discipline; whereas Niebuhr is concerned about the sins of the strong who throw their weight around—they need to be checked, for the most part. They use their moralism as a weapon in throwing their weight around. These are quite different problems. I think it would be fair to say that while Niebuhr has been a very helpful counselor to people—there is nobody who has given more of his time to individuals and to families about particular personal problems, although he is not someone who is always involved in counseling—but you won't find much help in his writings on these problems. It doesn't seem to me that you do. He's almost always concerned about the other dimension of the problem of sin.

Question (Dr. Hutchison): Professor Bennett, since we are talking about aspects of Niebuhr that haven't adequately

JOHN C. BENNETT

gotten into his writings, it does seem to me that, while his writings have been dominantly the economic and political, his appreciation of other aspects and facets of culture is an aspect of his thought that has come out more in his formal teaching and counseling.

Professor Bennett: Yes, I think that's true.

Question (Professor Robert McAfee Brown): Would you clarify one point about his treatment of Brunner's illustration about the judge. It seems to me that Brunner is saying that the judge is willing to do a good many evil things because he is finally justified by faith. Niebuhr took exception to the complacency of this. But in one sense, Isn't this really the predicament of the Christian, which Niebuhr would be the first to acknowledge? Everybody finds himself involved in doing many questionable and wrong things that some good may come; and as a final resource, I think he would say, "Lord, be merciful to me a sinner"—the final resource of forgiveness. How is this different from the situation of Brunner's judge?

Professor Bennett: Niebuhr reacts negatively to certain people, not so much against Brunner; but he does react rather quickly, and he re-acts too quickly on this. After all Brunner was talking about the judge who might stretch the law as far as possible, and yet, there were limits to his stretching of it. Even though it was an unjust law he did have limits. The judge could resign, of course; but there is a real problem there. Niebuhr was assuming the judge was made a little insensitive because of justification by faith. I use this to illustrate his impatience with the way in which these Christians of piety use justification. You will agree with that, of course.

Question (Father Robert Johann): Would you say that absolute values are real for him only insofar as they find insertion in a wider pragmatism?

Professor Bennett: This wider pragmatism, if you call it that, is also seen in the setting of certain permanent values that must be embodied in a good society. The only flexibility comes in how these are ordered and the priority among them. There is indefinite flexibility here. I would say that when it comes to a showdown his thought isn't so different from the wise Catholic who uses a great deal of prudence to cement his values together. It is not so different as some of the terminology would indicate. It isn't that he is a relativist in the sense that he has no permanent guides. Equal justice, or justice that is always being criticized by equality, is a very important guide right straight through.

Doctor Wieman: I wasn't clear on the first criticism you seemed to suggest. I thought it was along the lines in which I have also questioned him, but I'm not clear. I miss in Niebuhr a clear formulation of a standard for judging right and wrong and in indicating the direction for which history and society should move. It cannot be love; but that is too irrelevant. Niebuhr would probably say it cannot be a balance of power; that all depends upon where the fulcrum lies. You can have an evil balance of power, and justice—I don't really find a formula in his mind that could be applicable universally. The fact that people behind the Iron Curtain and people in other parts of the world do not find guidance would indicate that he hadn't really formulated a standard that is universally applicable.

Professor Bennett: I think his emphasis upon justice, constantly criticized by the principle of equality, would apply behind the Iron Curtain and everywhere. Just because it would be covered up by a propaganda line behind the Iron Curtain doesn't mean it is not applicable.

Professor Wieman: But equality, what is equality? How would you define equality?

Professor Bennett: As I did in my remarks earlier—it's a principle of criticism so that every particular structure of things, which tends to be set up for the sake of the powerful group in it, always needs to be broken up, always needs to be criticized. It's a dynamic thing, it's not sameness. The reason I use the men and women illustration is because it indicates where you can't have sameness, but mutual respect. You can have equal dignity, you can have freedom for all the external advantages which are the result of somebody's desire to keep his power. And that's what I mean by equality, and I think that's what he means. In fact, when it comes to this sort of thing, my own thought is so much molded by his, that when I say what I say, and he says what he says, there is not too much difference. I think that would be what he would think of equality. This would be applicable everywhere: equality of opportunity, impartiality before the law so that all people are treated equally in that context, but particularly the criticism of—I think you get at Niebuhr negatively so much better than you do positively. That's the reason that there's lack of vision in a way, lack of a positive vision. It's the criticism of inequality that's more obvious than the actual vision of what an equal world would be like.

Question (Professor Daniel Day Williams): Also, isn't freedom a correlative principle?

Professor Bennett: Yes, I think it always is. In fact, in some of his recent writings he has emphasized the danger that equality may smother freedom. Always you have these balancings—order, freedom and justice.

Question (Dr. Heimann): Then Doctor Wieman's question remains unanswered?

Professor Bennett: I think it remains unanswered in terms of pattern. That's true.

Question (Dr. John MacKay): Would you say that the basic characteristic of Niebuhr's thought, and perhaps one of its greatest limitations, is his rejection of any kind of absolute either for thought or behaviour; for thought, for example, in the rejection of any absolute of an ontological kind, e.g., the new man of the classical Christian tradition, however variant the types and forms of behaviour may be. In that connection also is his rejection of a basic divine plan or purpose to which life can be absolutely devoted. On the other hand, the limitation becomes evident today in the midst of our turmoil and anxiety, that youth coming on does not find that kind of absolute to which they must devote themselves. Behind the Iron Curtain, they are so bewildered that they don't find anything of that kind to which they can give themselves, even despairingly—but give themselves. Now the question that one raises is whether, as regards the eternal, if we take that seriously, or as regards the contemporary, life in the contemporary world, both in thought and action, can only be guided by an utter dedication to an absolute even when one is aware of the limitations of the self and leave the rest to God and history.

Professor Bennett: The more you make that absolute into a pattern, or the more it becomes a pattern, the more it is likely to be corrupted very quickly. However, I agree with the point that Father LaFarge made, that the lack of a pattern about which people can become greatly excited or to which they can become devoted is certainly here. Now there is an absolute norm and inspiration in the gospel; in the cross, in the revelation of God in Christ, there is this absolute norm. And then there are these landmarks that I have talked about, this love, and justice, and freedom. There are present a number of these landmarks, but you can't combine them into a pattern.

Question (Professor Wilhelm Pauck): But a vision is different from a pattern, isn't it?

Professor Bennett: I think at certain moments the vision could be articulated by Niebuhr, but he wouldn't want it to become the pattern for a group that organizes to impose this vision. He would be fearful of that.

Question (Dr. Gordon Harland): This afternoon Tillich mentioned that the situation in America meant that Niebuhr's understanding of sin became the most relevant, and that it was conditioned by that situation. I think that is true. I think one of the most exciting and most meaningful dimensions of Niebuhr's thought is precisely the doctrine of grace, as it is clarified in social terms and made relevant. I see this as a clarification of the insights and the observations into the nature of political reality, the dynamics of history; and the nature of man; but also the resources of spirit that is ever drawing out such truths as tolerance, humility, conscience, and faith. It's precisely this dimension of his thought that is most relevant for a generation that had so many other things to teach than the reality of sin.

Professor Bennett: Dr. Harland has written the best book about Niebuhr, entitled *The Thought of Reinhold Niebuhr,* at least the best book so far. We have another author here. I would say that he is a good person to answer this question: whether there is this vision or not. Do you think there is this invigorating vision? Is there not something lacking there?

Dr. Harland: I do not think there is a complete vision of the world order. I would like to know if anyone else has found it.

Professor Robert McAfee Brown: It seems to me that this would suggest—in terms of Doctor Heimann's concern that not too much is said to those behind the Iron Curtain— that this is most clearly articulated in the concern with grace and that perhaps this comes out best in the sermons. The sermons are that which will have the most significant word to say to the church in peril, and also the second volume of *The Nature and Destiny of Man.*

Canon Landon: We should mention here *Beyond Tragedy,* a great book of sermons in which Niebuhr gives us the comfort of a reasonable, religious, and holy hope.

HANS J. MORGENTHAU:

*The Influence of Reinhold Niebuhr
in American Political Life and Thought*

HANS J. MORGENTHAU:

When Professor Bennett, at the beginning of his lecture, commented on the structure of this Colloquium, I was reminded of the structure of the Barthian system—from the top to bottom. We have certainly now reached the bottom, dealing with so mundane a matter as politics, and probably we also have reached the bottom in terms of intellectual content and presentation.

In Jacob Burckhardt's, *The History of the Renaissance in Italy*, there is a chapter entitled, "The Rediscovery of Man." I think if one would want to bring into one formula the contribution which Reinhold Niebuhr has made to the political thinking and the political life of America, one could say that he is responsible for the rediscovery of Political Man. He has rediscovered Political Man in five different respects: He has rediscovered the autonomy of the political sphere. He has rediscovered the intellectual dilemma of understanding politics and acting within the political sphere. He has rediscovered the moral dilemma of political action. He has restored the organic relationship between political thought and political action. Finally, he has rediscovered the tragedy which is inherent in the political act.

HANS J. MORGENTHAU

The Rediscovery of Political Man

We are all aware of the tendency in our culture to look at politics, domestic and international, as a derivative of something else, and more particularly of economics. On this the nineteenth-century Liberals and the Marxists have seen eye to eye. Both believe that the lust for power, the Augustinian *animus dominandi,* is nothing more than a symptom of a passing phase of human history. The Liberals would attribute it to the atavistic institutions of feudalism and aristocratic rule; the Marxists, of course, would attribute it to the class society. Herbert Spencer, for instance, thought that while aristocracies waged war in order to satisfy their competitive instincts, industrial societies would satisfy those instincts through business competition, investments, and speculation at the Stock Exchange.

It is this kind of optimistic denial of the intrinsic relationship of the lust for power and its social upshot—the political sphere—which Reinhold Niebuhr has destroyed, and he has restored the idea which was basic both to the Biblical and the ancient Greek and Roman conception of Man: that the 'lust for power' and the social configurations to which that lust gives rise is an intrinsic element, an intrinsic quality of human nature itself. It cannot be reformed out of existence. There is no phase of history which will not show it. There is no social organization which will not bear the mark of it. This, it seems to me, is the first political lesson we can derive from Reinhold Niebuhr.

The understanding of politics is, in a sense, nothing

more than the understanding of history brought up to date. It is here that we are confronted again with a strong tendency in our culture which tries to destroy the autonomy of history and politics within the intellectual sphere; which, in other words, tries to assimilate the historic process to the processes of nature. You see this tendency predominant in philosophy and history as well as in the mundane research enterprises of many of our universities, generally well supported by rich foundations. They say, "Here lies the salvation," and try to apply what they think are the methods of the natural sciences to the social scene. Reinhold Niebuhr has time and again made emphatically the point that the historic area—the social scene—is essentially different from nature, and that the intellectual methods which are capable of understanding politics and society in general are bound to be different from the methods which apply to the discovery of the secret of nature.

Here we are face to face with an essentially insoluble problem to which Reinhold Niebuhr has pointed also time and again, that is, the conjunction of uniformities and contingencies. History is a mass of events which, in certain respects, show uniformities from which certain laws, certain general principles, can be derived. But it is also a mass of contingencies, of unique events which happen in that way only once and never again. The problem, which can only be adumbrated but cannot be solved once and for all, is how to assess the weight of the unique, the contingent, as over against the weight of the repetitive, the uniform. It is by virtue of the insolubility of this task that all philosophies of history, all predictions in politics have come ultimately to nought. For when we ask, for instance, what are Khrushchev's intentions with regard to Berlin, we are confronted with a number of limited alternatives which constitute the rational aspects of the situation, which allow us to arrive at certain general principles and conclusions with regard to them. We are, on the other hand, confronted with uncertainties, with unfathomable factors, which make it impossible for us to arrive at anything more certain than a series of hunches as to which of the limited number of alternatives is likely to come to pass. So the intellectual problem with which politics confronts us is essentially insoluble beyond a series of hunches which only the future will prove to be correct or incorrect. It is this teaching of Niebuhr which has naturally given rise to a great deal of dissatisfaction and criticism, some of which we have heard this afternoon (and I shall return to the problem in a moment.)

The moral problem, the moral dilemma of politics, has perhaps been more distorted by our culture than any other fundamental problem of politics. The moral problem of politics is posed by the inescapable discrepancy between the commands of Christian teaching, of Christian ethics, and the requirements of political success. It is impossible, if I may put it in somewhat extreme and striking terms, to be a successful politician and a good Christian. This juxtaposition, this assumption of an inescapable conflict between the teachings of Christian ethics and the requirements of political success is, of course, unpalatable to the man in the street; and some of those streets run through American campuses. Thus American society—and I should say not only American society but Western civilization in general—has devised two different methods, two different intellectual instruments, by which it has tried to reconcile the commands of Christian ethics and the requirements of successful political action. Either it has reinterpreted the teachings of Christian ethics in a "liberal" way, in a way which is conducive to justifying and rationalizing the political act so that the gap between the two is narrowed by changing the commands of Christian ethics; or else the political act is made to appear as something different from what it actually is, as something nicer, less sinful than it actually is, and thereby the gap is narrowed. Thus the political sphere tends to be surrounded with what you might call a moralistic halo so that both the majesty of the moral law and the starkness of the political act disappear in this kind of compromise between the commands of ethics and the requirements of successful political action. It is this moralism, so common a prejudice in our society, against which Reinhold Niebuhr has argued so often and with so much critical success.

It has been said this afternoon, by way of what I suspect to be a mild criticism, that Reinhold Niebuhr's political thought is lacking in vision, and that it is tied to the particular circumstances of our political scene so that it has nothing to give, for instance, to the people behind the Iron Curtain. I should say in defense of Reinhold Niebuhr's political thought that this organic relationship between political philosophy and a particular historic situation or concrete political problem is by no means accidental. It is, so it seems to me, a prerequisite for creative political thought. For all the great political philosophers, whom you remember because they are great, have developed their political thought in connection with a concrete practical political problem. The way we are dealing with political philosophy in our universities, for instance, is certainly not the way in which great political philosophies have actually been developed. They have been developed, you may say, in a controversial way, and from Plato and Aristotle to Marx and Lenin it was on the basis of concrete political problems waiting to be solved that political thought developed. *The Federalist,* for instance, the most distinguished document of American political philosophy, was the result of a very practical political problem, the ratification of the Constitution, and the supporters of ratification wrote articles for newspapers arguing in favor of ratification. So it is really no argument to say that Reinhold Niebuhr, because he has dealt with the concrete political problems of the day in a concrete manner, has thereby failed in his calling as a great political philosopher.

It is, of course, true that nothing follows directly from what Reinhold Niebuhr has said about civil liberties, or race relations, or any other concrete problem of American politics, for the problems of Poland, Czechoslovakia, or China. But behind that concrete treatment of concrete political problems lies a general political philosophy, a set of general political principles, which have inspired that concrete treatment of concrete problems and which are of universal applicability. In other words, the method, the approach, of Reinhold Niebuhr as a political philosopher is not in essence different from—let me say—Edmund Burke's approach, who writes a letter to the electors of Bristol explaining to them what he is supposed to do as their representative—certainly as much a local and parochial problem as you can imagine. But Burke treats this problem in such a way that that letter becomes the classic philosophic exposition of one of the fundamental principles of representative government. If one tried to judge Reinhold Niebuhr's contribution to political philosophy by such standards, I think one would arrive at a more positive conclusion than if one asks whether what Reinhold Niebuhr has said to us about our political problems has a direct relevance for the problems of other people. Certainly what Edmund Burke wrote to the electors of Bristol, in itself, had only relevance for the electors of Bristol; it was a local matter. But behind and within that concrete disposition of a concrete problem there was a general political philosophy. And so it is, I think, with the political thought of Reinhold Niebuhr.

It has also been said in criticism that there is in the political thought of Reinhold Niebuhr no indication for future political action, that there is no vision of a "brave new world" or of a political program upon which we are to embark tomorrow and the day after. Again this is not by accident, and in a sense, so it seems to me, perhaps out of my personal sympathy for this kind of approach to politics, it is the mark of a profound understanding of the limits of political action that there is no such over-all vision, no such program to be found in the political thought of Reinhold Niebuhr. It has been mentioned by different speakers, and quite correctly, that Reinhold Niebuhr's political thought has an essentially pragmatic quality; but so has political action. Political action itself proceeds in small steps of which the consequences can either not be foreseen at all, or are only visible in the vaguest and dimmest outlines. No great political deed has been accomplished on the basis of a great vision of what the future would hold, or if it has, whatever actually came out of the deed was entirely different from what the vision anticipated.

There is, I think, in Reinhold Niebuhr's political thought a self-limitation which is the very reflection of the subject matter of politics. It is the awareness, to put it in different words, of the tragic character of the political act. We plan a political strategy in order to achieve a certain result, but the result, more often than not, has only a very remote relation to what we intend. This is the ruse of the idea of which Hegel spoke. And if you look, for instance, at the most consistent modern attempt to put a political vision into practice on the basis of rather profound insights into the nature of man and society—I am referring, of course, to Marxism—you realize to what extent the results belie the vision and the intent. So it is here again that I would say that the Niebuhrian awareness of the limits of the human mind with regard to the political act is not a shortcoming in a political philosopher, but it is rather the expression of the very nature of politics itself.

The Problem of Nuclear War

Another criticism of Niebuhr's political thought which has been mentioned this afternoon concerns the problem of nuclear war. If I understood the debate correctly, the suggestion was made that Reinhold Niebuhr has changed his mind, that he has been inconsistent. I don't believe that at all. Again it is probably by virtue of the similarity between the development of my own thought and that of Niebuhr's with regard to this fundamental problem that I can speak with a certain degree of confidence in trying to interpret the position of Niebuhr.

There is a fundamental difference between the dropping of the first two atomic bombs on Hiroshima and Nagasaki, on the one hand, and all-out nuclear war, on the other. The initiation of the atomic age through these two events still retained a rational relationship between the use of violence as a means and the ends of foreign policy. This rational relationship has been radically destroyed through the possibility of all-out nuclear war, for a war—that is, the use of violence as a means to the ends of foreign policy—which destroys the parties to the dispute as well as the object of the dispute is an utter absurdity. I am not arguing that we are not going to be forced to make this absurdity come true. But it is an absurdity, nevertheless. So it is not that Reinhold Niebuhr's mind has changed, but that the age has changed upon which Reinhold Niebuhr has brought to bear his insights into politics. Thus it is perfectly consistent to defend, from a political and moral point of view, the dropping of the first two atomic bombs as rational means to the ends of foreign policy, and to deny the rationality and the moral validity of all-out nuclear war.

The Problem of Political Ideologies

Let me say, finally, a few words about a central problem of politics on which new light has been shed in Niebuhr's book *The Structure of Nations and Empires*. This is the problem of political ideologies. It is here that the distortion of the truth about politics and political degradation of ethical values is most evident, and has had the most serious consequences for our understanding of politics and our evaluation of ethical principles. Since—if I may summarize very sketchily Niebuhr's thought on that—the aspiration for power and the struggle for power arising from conflicting aspirations have a negative moral connotation in our society: those who seek power, that is to say, those who are engaged in the business of politics, must make it appear that what they are aiming at is something different than power, something more noble, something more worthy of moral approval than power. Thus political ideologies, the intellectual concealment and transformation of the political act into something different from what it actually is, is a necessary concomitant of the political act itself, for it is one of the preconditions for political success. And so we find on the highest level of political organization, the level of empires and churches, that the latter take on the aspect of empire by striving for power in order to maintain themselves and to expand, and that the empires, on the other hand, drape themselves in a paraphernalia of religion in order to justify their existence and policies in terms of morality and divine providence rather than of power. Reinhold Niebuhr has shown that this is not a quality which certain political parties or certain nations possess while others are free from them, but rather that this relationship between a concealed political reality and a corrupted ethic is of the very essence of politics; that, in other words, political ideologies are an inevitable weapon in the struggle for power which all participants must use to a greater or lesser extent.

Let me say in conclusion that I have always considered Reinhold Niebuhr the greatest living political philosopher of America, perhaps the only creative political philosopher since Calhoun. It is indicative of the very nature of American politics and of our thinking about matters political that it is not a statesman, not a practical politician, let alone a professor of political science or of philosophy, but a theologian who can claim this distinction of being the greatest living political philosopher of America. For we have had a tendency as a people—one that goes back to the eighteenth century—to take our political institutions for granted, to regard them as the best there could be, which need no philosophic justification or intellectual elaboration. It is not by accident that it was on the occasion of the great conflict which led to the Civil War that a great political philosophy was developed in order to justify a particular position within the American political system. So it was unlikely, in view of the normal operations of the American political system—the lack of sharp and stratified class distinctions and of fundamental and permanent conflicts—that there should arise a political philosophy from within secular political society. It needed a man who could look at American society, as it were, from the outside—*sub specie aeternitatis*—to develop such a political philosophy; and that man, I think, is Reinhold Niebuhr.

DISCUSSION:

Col. Francis Miller: Professor Morgenthau, I would like to make a comment rather than ask a question. I'm rather distressed by the emphases you've made, and I'm not sure they entirely do Niebuhr justice. I happen to be a poor Christian. I am also a politician. I have fought in the toughest political league in the United States for 25 years, and I know something about it. What I want to say with all the emphasis at my command is that it is no more difficult to be a Christian in politics in the Southern states than it is to be a Christian minister. I fact, I think it is more difficult to be a minister and a Christian, than it is to be a politician and a Christian. At any rate, it is as difficult to be a manufacturer and a Christian, or a second-hand car salesman and a Christian, or a banker and a Christian, as it is to be a politician and a Christian. Now I feel very deeply about this, and that's the reason I want to say it. I wish Reinhold Niebuhr were here, because I love him very much. The emphasis you've made tonight is in effect saying to young men: If you're going to be Christians, you're going to find it very difficult to be one in the political arena. That leads on to the last thing you said:

that politics is essentially a struggle for power. In one sense, of course, it is. But I know men who have gone down into the political arena who knew they couldn't win, who never expected to win, and who consequently could never exercise power, but who knew, by the grace of God, that if they stated what they believed, and appealed to the conscience of the people, and fought for some great cause, that out of that some better day might come, and that in losing, they might make a greater political contribution, Dr. Morgenthau, than in winning power.

Professor Morgenthau: I want to say two things about this: I would have no quarrel with your statement that it is difficult to be a Christian to begin with. But I would still maintain that it is particularly difficult to be a Christian in politics, because the aim of man in politics is to dominate another man, to use a man as an instrument, as a means to his ends; and this is a direct denial of Judaeo-Christian ethics. The political act is in a specific, particularly acute sense incompatible with Christian ethics, in a sense in which the non-political act is free. As concerns the self-sacrifice of the political actor who acts knowing that he can't win, he operates in a political context in which his defeat becomes an element in ultimate victory, so that indirectly his defeat aims at the political victory which he cannot obtain, but somebody else will.

Dr. Eduard Heimann: I have some rather serious objections to announce, but I do not want to do it without first saying that I much admire the speech we have just heard by a man who has come to an alliance with Reinhold Niebuhr without being his pupil. Here are two movements, two ideas, moving closer and closer together until there is a kind of identification. There is shown so beautifully and so modestly in what Dr. Morgenthau has presented just now. . . . I have four or five points which I want to speak about briefly.

First, as to the Christian statesman, what is a Christian here? In my understanding, a Christian is a sinner who knows that he is one; if I am a Christian in political life, I know that I am a sinner in political life. I do not see what would be the difference between a Christian in political life and anywhere else. I think Colonel Miller was right when he said that a minister is in a very bad position because Christianity is a vested interest with him. For a professor, the truth is a vested interest, and it is very difficult to serve a cause which happens to coincide with your vested interest. This is the predicament, it seems to me, of the preacher and of the professor. That is my first point. This being so, there is a Christian statesman of the very highest level of whom we all know. His name is Abraham Lincoln, and Niebuhr, for once, would agree with me on that, sir. . . . You don't seem to agree on this. . . .

Professor Morgenthau: I would agree on that too, but he is a unique figure in history, he is completely atypical.

Dr. Heimann: Yes he is a unique figure but . . . this is a human possibility as Lincoln has shown.

Now my second point. It was I who raised that objection or doubt as to whether the things which Niebuhr said in such eloquent words could in any way be used by people behind the Iron Curtain. This is the reason why even in Western Germany his influence is always under a cloud: it is spoken from the happy position of a man in the Western world to his fellows, without regard to the other side. When you say, sir, that this is how a political idea, a political philosophy arises, you are quite right. I did not speak of the political philosopher. I did speak of the preacher and the theologian, and it seems to me that a preacher who has nothing to say to those on the other side, being a political philosopher of a certain kind, falls down in this regard, not on his political mission, but on his ethical and theological mission. That was my second point.

My third point is this. When it comes to the strategy in the cold war, which, of course, is behind all of this, the Iron Curtain is precisely the limit of the applicability of his thought. This was also, I said, the reason why Barth, being only a preacher for the Church, can be used by the people who have nothing to cling to but the Church. Kant, whom I do not follow in every respect, made a very wise observation in his teachings, i.e., you must never make war in such a way as to make it impossible to make peace. I have never come across in Niebuhr's teachings any idea on how he thinks the Cold War could be settled. Except for more recent reservations on the violence in this struggle, I have never seen any structural idea on how this could be done. I haven't seen anybody who could, but if there is a great man like Reinhold Niebuhr—I am greatly convinced that there is no greater—then I would have hoped that he might have something to say to us which he has failed to say. Now I retract because I am not in the position to fill that gap either.

Now the fourth point is, however, that the pragmatic approach, with which you are also very closely identified —and this is primarily, of course, a bridge between the two of you—is always good within the structure, but not beyond. It is the structural analysis, rather than the pragmatic, which is to a certain extent missing in his profound analyses. He says that here is right, there is wrong, in the position of this man; he says here is right, there is wrong, in the position of his adversary. All this is admirable in a given situation. So if you permit me, I will give an example of the criticism I have against Niebuhr's politics. My example is the Suez problem, where the two of you were identified with the English-French attack on Egypt; and we all for moralistic reasons—more or less, maybe—were against it; and I do not think the reasons were—certainly not in my case, because I had written against it—purely moralistic; they were structural. There was a new situation arising which had to be anticipated by a wise strategist, and had not been. For in the situation as it was, England and France might have been right; but in the situation as it would be tomorrow, they would be profoundly wrong. This is a world in which structures are changing more rapidly than could be mastered in a pragmatic way. The old countries, the powerful countries, must know that they are interdependent with the new, and that there is no such thing as national sovereignty. Why? Because there are the powerful and the not powerful, the rich and the not rich, and both competing in the same world market for the same scarce goods; one group with much purchasing power, the other with little purchasing power. That these latter have little purchasing power is the fault of those who have failed to develop them as long as they had them in their imperial hands. Now this is a structural point which I have missed in the discussions. I do not think that the wisest political philosopher of our day is wise enough on all points.

Professor Morgenthau: The last point is certainly unexceptionable. To come back to your other points . . . and particularly to the alleged failing of Reinhold Niebuhr as a preacher. St. Paul didn't preach to everybody but only to the Corinthians, the Romans, or the Ephesians, addressing himself to their concrete situations. And it was again the relevance of the insights he brought to bear upon the concrete situations which gave Paul his influence. I think the same is true of Reinhold Niebuhr. There is beneath Niebuhr's concrete discussion of concrete problems a general philosophy (which is of universal applicability), elaborating the worth and dignity of the individual, the balancing of powers within the State, the guarantee of the freedom of all through pitting the power of one against the power of the other, and so forth.

Professor Henry N. Wieman: I think perhaps your criticism was directed also to what I said this afternoon. At any rate I want to speak a little upon the point. I agree with you that Reinhold Niebuhr is a great political philosopher and I greatly admire his criticisms. I want to add also that I greatly admire your own criticism, those that I've read of political practices of our own country in international situations. But no man is omniscient, infallible and perfect in all areas of thought, and it seems to me that Niebuhr is less clear and articulate on the general principles that should guide our lives. Every concrete situation has to be treated in its own context, as you say, and we never know what is the right thing to do because of the complexity of the situation. But there are general principles which are such, sir, that what one seeks to promote in one situation should not conflict with what he seeks to promote in other situations; or what one seeks to promote in one age, should not conflict with what should be sought in other ages. There must be general principles which run through all concrete situations and all periods in history which we may not know with any clarity at all, but the attempt to formulate them is one great problem, it seems to me, in politics as well as elsewhere; and Reinhold Niebuhr's greatness lies, it seems to me, not in formulating those most general principles, but rather in criticizing a concrete situation.

Professor Morgenthau: I would fully agree with that. This is what makes him a great political philosopher rather than a great philosopher.

Canon Landon: It seems appropriate to conclude with Reinhold Niebuhr's own words from a recent issue of *Christianity and Crisis*, where he was discussing the resumption of nuclear testing: "Modern history has moved into the eschatological dimension in which all our judgments are made under the shadow of the final judgment. May the Lord have mercy on our souls."

The Response of Reinhold Niebuhr

REINHOLD NIEBUHR:

It is somewhat embarrassing to make a response to the analyses of my thought by three good friends, chiefly because they are so extravagant in their estimate of the significance of my labors. One suspects that either friendship has dulled their critical faculties or that they have concluded that a colloquium about the thought of an aged colleague is so much like a funeral that the axiom applies: "About the dead speak nothing but good."

In answering Professor Bennett's comprehensive analysis of my thought and my activity in the field of social ethics, I can only conclude that his systematic mind has given me the benefit of the doubt and made my thought more systematic and coherent than it really is. I also must confess to bewilderment in reading his record of my organizational activities, for the record reveals a certain lack of a sense of proportion, and an inclination to flee from the hard tasks of serious thought to the easier responsibilities of organization. Many of the hours devoted to committee meetings were no doubt necessary, but with the wisdom of hindsight I now realize that many of those hours might have been devoted to serious reflection. They could have saved me from an inferiority complex, as I lived for years among devoted scholars without the competence of a scholar.

Professor Tillich accurately reports the constant dialogue in which we engaged in regard to the proper way of describing the human situation of radical freedom of the spirit and the corruption of that freedom by man's undue self-concern. He accurately reports the conversations we had at Harvard before the Colloquium, in which I confessed that I had made a mistake in hurling the traditional symbols of Christian realism—the fall and original sin—in the teeth of modern culture when I sought to criticize the undue optimism of the culture. Both these symbols, though historically significant, are subject to misunderstanding in a secular culture. So much time is spent in clearing up misapprehensions that it would be more economical simply to describe the paradox of man's freedom and its corruption by the mastery of the anxious self over the rational capacities, which in the theory of the Enlightenment, guaranteed man's virtue, because it was assumed that they were the masters, and not the instruments, of the self. I still think that Paul Tillich's translation of these symbols into the ontological terms *essential* and *existential* man is too Plotinian in that it implies, if not asserts, that the whole temporal process is a corruption of the eternal. Thereby one precious Biblical concept, embodied in the idea of the goodness of creation, may be obscured. I would now rather translate these historic symbols into descriptive, rather than ontological, terms.

In regard to Professor Morgenthau's analysis of my political philosophy and the resultant discussion, I would be tempted to try to eliminate some cause of debate by amending the statement by Professor Morgenthau, admitted by him to be "in striking and extreme terms," namely, the statement that it is "impossible to be a successful politician and good Christian." Morgenthau is concerned, as I am, to dispel the illusions of all forms of liberalism, which seek to obscure the fact that the political order must concern itself with interest and with power. This concern makes it necessary to call attention to the moral ambiguity of the political order and the consequent impossibility of making a pure ethic relevant in this realm. But if one speaks of the "discrepancy between the commands of Christian teaching and the requirements of political success," one may concede too much to the perfectionist versions of Christianity, some of which make so much of this discrepancy that the Mennonites, for instance, specifically declare the responsibilities of the magistrate to be incompatible with the Christian life. But "Christian teaching" ought to include more than the absolute demands of the Sermon on the Mount. A Christian faith which accurately portrays the selfishness of men, as well as their capacity for justice, is bound to insist not only on the freedom of the conscience of the individual, but also on the right of the community to be guarded against the peril of the individual's greed or lust to power.

Christian teaching must include not only the love commandment but the norms of justice which can and must be instruments of the love commandment; and which may be drawn from the prophets of Israel or from the classical sources from which Catholicism drew them. It should, therefore, provide the vocation of the politician or statesman who moves in the vast and morally ambiguous realm of the political community with as much integrity as possible, and with an humble awareness of the taint in all competitive positions in the political spectrum. There should be a place in "the kingdom of God" for men like Abraham Lincoln, or even for the rather too self-righteous idealists such as William Gladstone and Woodrow Wilson, not to speak of all the rest of us who in some degree handle power, responsibility, and interest in some community or other.

I do not think we will sacrifice any value in the "realist" approach to the political order, of which Morgenthau is such an eminent and acknowledged exponent, and to which I am personally deeply indebted, if we define the moral ambiguity of the political realm in terms which do not rob it of moral content.

I suspect that such a reformulation, which my friend Morgenthau would probably accept as his description of the moral situation as admittedly "extreme," would meet many of Francis Miller's objections. They ought to be met, because Miller's long experience in state politics proves there is room to be creative in the political realm by men of integrity and courage.

I am not certain that anything which I might do to amend or explain the position which Morgenthau and I have in common could quiet the criticism of my old friend Eduard Heimann. I am a pragmatist who tries to be guided in pragmatic judgments by the general principles of justice as they have developed in Western culture. But I know of no principles which could guide us in choosing between various emphases on various competing or complementary principles, according to the weight they are given by historical contingencies. I know of no general principle, Christian or otherwise, which will solve the cold war and the nuclear dilemma. I agree with Morgenthau that if this should be the responsibility of philosophy, it is certainly not the task of political philosophy. A Christian engaged in political philosophy can do no more than seek to prevent premature solutions of essentially insoluble problems, hoping that time will make some solutions possible tomorrow which are not possible today.

Let me conclude by a word of gratitude to the three distinguished friends for their thoughtful papers, and to all the friends who honored me by the care and graciousness with which they examined my thought.

NOTES:

Editor's Introduction

1. Reinhold Niebuhr, *Beyond Tragedy* (New York: Scribner's, 1937), p. x.
2. *Ibid.*, pp. 3 and 24.
3. *Ibid.*, p. 114.
4. Paul Scherer in *Reinhold Niebuhr, His Religious, Social and Political Thought,* ed. Kegley and Bretall (New York: Macmillan, 1956), p. 322.
5. The Book of Common Prayer, Articles of Religion, No. IX.
6. Reinhold Niebuhr, *The Structure of Nations and Empires* (New York: Scribner's, 1959), pp. 7; 298-9.
7. Paul Tillich, *The Protestant Era* (University of Chicago Press, 1948), Chapter XIV.
8. Paul Tillich, *The New Being,* (New York: Scribner's, 1955), p. 88.
9. Niebuhr, *Beyond Tragedy,* p. 64.
10. *Ibid.*, p. 62.
11. Paul Tillich, *op. cit.*
12. Reinhold Niebuhr, *Moral Man and Immoral Society* (New York: Scribner's, 1937), pp. 276-277.
13. Niebuhr, *Beyond Tragedy,* pp. 109-110.

NOTES

Paul Tillich: Sin and Grace in the Theology of Reinhold Niebuhr

1. Charles Hartshorne, "Tillich's Doctrine of God" in *The Theology of Paul Tillich*, Kegley and Bretall, eds. (New York: Macmillan).

John Bennett: Reinhold Niebuhr's Contribution to Christian Social Ethics

1. Reinhold Niebuhr, *The Nature and Destiny of Man* (New York: Scribner's, 1943), II, 122.
2. *Ibid.*, II, 85.
3. *Ibid.*, II, 197.
4. *Ibid.*, II, 196.
5. *Ibid.*, II, 284.
6. *Ibid.*, II, 268.
7. Reinhold Niebuhr, *The Children of Light and the Children of Darkness* (New York: Scribner's, 1944), p. xi.
8. *The Nature and Destiny of Man*, II, 247.
9. Reinhold Niebuhr, *Faith and History* (New York: Scribner's, 1949), p. 185.
10. *The Nature and Destiny of Man*, II, 248.
11. *Ibid.*, II, 254.
12. Harrison Brown and James Real, *The Community of Fear* (Santa Barbara, California: Fund of the Republic, 1958). Introduction by Reinhold Niebuhr, pp. 4-5.
13. Niebuhr, *Foreign Policy and the Free Society*, p. 67.
14. Reinhold Niebuhr, "The Nuclear Dilemma—a Discussion" in *Christianity and Crisis*, November 13, 1961, p. 202.

www.ingramcontent.com/pod-product-compliance
Lightning Source LLC
Chambersburg PA
CBHW050839160426
43192CB00011B/2080